Mechanised Warfare in Color

MILITARY TRANSPORT
of World War II
including Post War Vehicles

by
CHRIS ELLIS

illustrated by
DENIS BISHOP

THE MACMILLAN COMPANY
NEW YORK, N.Y.

THE MACMILLAN COMPANY
866 Third Avenue, New York, N.Y. 10022

First published in Great Britain in 1971 by
Blandford Press Ltd., London

Library of Congress Catalog Card Number: 70-152283
First American Edition 1971

Printed in Great Britain

CONTENTS

PREFACE

This volume in the 'Mechanised Warfare in Color' series is a direct continuation of our previous book 'Military Transport of World War I'. Despite its conveniently definitive title the earlier volume covered a generous period of history both before and after World War I, right up to 1939 in fact, so that all the major and important developments of the inter-war period could be described. Because development in World War II was so intensive—it was an almost wholly mechanised war—the greater part of this present book describes vehicles produced in the 1940–45 period. Towards the end, however, we have presented some of the vehicles produced in the 25 years since the war ended, mainly to show types developed either as a result of the lessons of World War II or as replacements for famous wartime types.

Most of the vehicles built in the 1939–45 period were produced concurrently so that it is almost impossible to present any kind of chronological order. Similarly many of the types of the 1930s which were described in the previous book continued in production and/or service throughout World War II and beyond. A date is given with each description which serves as a guide to a vehicle's development or introduction, but generally everything shown here was in service for the duration of the war and often well into the 1950s or even later. In fact the convention of conveniently compartmentalising the subject into periods is not strictly valid for military vehicles since, with the exception of very short lulls immediately after both world wars, development of new models has continued just as rapidly as commercial vehicle development. Most armed services therefore have, at any one time, vehicles in service which span a development period of 20 years or more. In 1955, for instance, the British Army still had in service a few AEC Marshals of decidedly vintage appearance, a type which had entered service in 1935 and is described in the previous volume. As these words are written in 1971 I know of a couple of Bedford water tankers still in daily service at an overseas British Army base after 27 years service, even though the model concerned has not been shown on any official vehicle inventory for many years. Cases of American-built vehicles still in common service with various armies after a quarter of a century are almost legion—the DUKW, for example, described in this book being still a standard service type with several armies including the British and West German. Similarly the Korean War of 1950–53 and the Suez Campaign of 1956 were fought almost entirely with World War II period equipment, so it would not be entirely correct to think of the 1940–45 vehicles described here as being rigidly confined to World War II service.

There are a number of cross-references in this book referred to as plate numbers— e.g. 'see plate 106'. These correspond to the relevant numbered drawings but it should also be understood that this includes reference to the appropriate descriptive text as well. Similarly there are a few cross-references to vehicles shown in the previous book but these are clearly identified as such in the text.

Both Denis Bishop and myself would like to thank Peter Chamberlain, the staff of the Imperial War Museum, London, Scammell Lorries, Ltd., Noel Ayliffe-Jones of British Leyland, and the Parachute Regiment Museum, Aldershot, all of whom assisted in various ways in the location of visual references for the drawings.

Finally I would like to thank Mrs. F. Watson for making such an excellent job of typing the manuscript.

CHRIS ELLIS
LONDON, 1971

INTRODUCTION

The World War of 1939–45 was the first almost wholly mechanised conflict in history. It involved the production of motor vehicles at a rate and on a scale not previously thought possible. During the war years there were four major producers of military road vehicles, the United States, Great Britain, Canada and Germany, and these four countries, naturally, set the pace in design and development. The French automotive industry, like the Czech and others, was virtually part of the German war effort for the duration, while the Italian, Japanese and Russian industries, not particularly big in peacetime, virtually carried on with building existing designs during the war years and introduced little that was new. In this volume, therefore, the vehicles of the four major producers predominate.

The United States built over 3,200,000 military vehicles during the World War II period, sufficient to equip not only the U.S. Army, but also a large part of the various Allied armies. By 1945, in the U.S. Army, there was one vehicle to every four men— in contrast to 1918 when, after a massive mechanisation programme the ratio was one vehicle to every 40 men. Before America entered the war in December, 1941 she was already involved as a major supplier of equipment to Britain and her Allies. In 1940 this was on a direct sales basis when France and Britain in particular were the major purchasers. Many vehicles ordered by France in 1939 were delivered to Britain instead after the fall of France, and after Dunkirk Britain made purchases to offset her heavy losses of equipment in the fighting in France and Flanders. In March 1941 the famous Lend-Lease Act became law which made equipment of all kinds, including military vehicles available on a much bigger scale than hitherto. Subsequently many thousands of vehicles were supplied to Britain and over 400,000 were sent to Soviet Russia where American types were in the majority on some fighting fronts.

Apart from the sheer size of the American truck industry in 1940, it was also the most advanced in terms of manufacturing methods and design. Also conditions in America, long distance haulage and a big commercial market made most American truck types fairly easily adaptable to military requirements. In fact, the majority of American military vehicles were of almost direct commercial origin and only a few types actually originated from purely military requirements—of these perhaps the Jeep DUKW, and the tracked LVTs and High Speed Tractors are the most obvious examples.

In pre-war days the procurement of military vehicle types was in the hands of the Quartermaster Corps and in peacetime relatively few vehicles were bought, and then mainly on competitive bidding for contracts from the motor industry. While standardisation of military types was always talked about, this was never achieved, for it was decided that to provide vehicles quickly in emergency it would be necessary to buy whatever were the most suitable designs from commercial builders. The only 'standardised' requirement was in the load classes laid down.

This policy meant that in 1940–41 when re-armament began on a massive scale, dozens of different makes were procured, albeit in standard load categories. This provided the numbers required fairly quickly but at the price of a storekeeper's nightmare, for an inventory of literally millions of spare parts was needed for maintenance. By 1941, negotiated contracts had replaced competitive bidding and in 1942 the original complications were greatly reduced by choosing the design of one manufacturer in each class and standardising on the one chassis. In August 1942, the responsibility for vehicle procurement was transferred to the Ordnance Department who subsequently took a much firmer control over production programmes and the supply of parts. Even so this did not prevent a few crises, notably the severe shortage of 'heavy-heavy' class trucks in the late war period, largely due to inadequate forward planning before the United States had any actual campaign experience.

Closely allied to the United States in a production sense was Canada who produced the impressive total of 815,729 motor vehicles in the years 1939–45. In this country subsidiaries of major United States automotive firms were well established and a fine range of trucks was produced combining American manufacturing expertise with British military requirements and specifications. More details of Canadian production are given with the individual vehicle histories.

In Britain the War Office had established design requirements in the 1920s and 1930s that were very precise and were originally still tied to a subsidy scheme. By the late 1930s the old requirement for six-wheel-chassis had been dropped and most of the new (i.e. late 1930s) designs were four-wheelers. Unlike the United States, there was no great commercial market in Britain for four-wheel-drive vehicles and development of this type was initiated entirely for military purposes in 1939. For most manufacturers this was a new class of vehicle. Other than that British designs were essentially refinements of pre-war types and had a good reputation for reliability and ruggedness. Because of the exacting War Department requirements for body sizes etc. and because there were fewer manufacturers, Britain did not get involved in any great battle for standardisation.

Germany learned the lesson about standardisation from the Americans well before the war. In the early 1930s the newly established German Army (Reichswehr) ordered vast numbers of specialised types of purpose-built vehicle, many of them expensive and too complicated for commercial use. In an effort to prevent the maintenance problems that were already looming, the 'Schell Programme' of 1938 made a clean sweep of the old production and design programmes (though vehicles of the pre-1938 era remained in service) and introduced a complete new series of standardised chassis designs for the different classes of vehicle. These were so 'standardised' that little more than the bonnets and badges remained to distinguish the different vehicle manufacturers. Like the Americans, too, the Germans produced a series of simple small vehicles of the 'field car' type which is, incidentally, one of the few new classes of everyday vehicle which came into being as a result of World War II designs.

In this book a more detailed account of development is given with the individual vehicle histories. What must be emphasised, however, is that the illustrations and entries given here represent only a fraction of the different makes and models produced in the period covered. Output was truly enormous and what we try to do is give a representative picture of what went on.

Designations

Where possible the original official designation or description has been used in this book. However, this was frequently either complicated or incomplete (often omitting the manufacturer's name for instance) and in such cases this has been added to the titles. Often there was no really fixed designation and in such cases a suitably descriptive one has been provided by the author, following the conventional style. The now universal chassis description is also used (whether used in connection with the original vehicle or not) which shows the total wheels and the driven wheels in the form (for example) 6 × 4—six wheels in all, of which four are driven. Thus 4 × 4 indicates four wheels in all, all driven.

1
Field Artillery Tractor, 4×4, Morris C8, U.K.

2
Field Artillery Tractor, 4×4, Ford (Canadian Military Pattern),
Canada/U.K.

3
Medium Artillery Tractor, 4×4, AEC Matador, U.K.

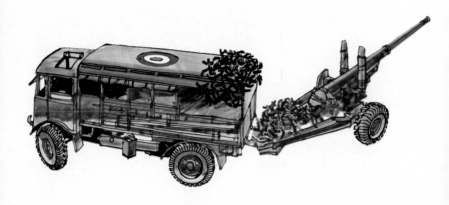

4
Medium Artillery Tractor, 4×4, AEC Matador with 5·5 inch gun-howitzer, U.K.

5
Flight Refueller, 2,500 gallon, 6×6, AEC 0854, U.K.

6
Flight Refueller, 2,500 gallon, 6×6, AEC 0854, U.K.

7
Truck, 3 ton, GS, 6×4, AEC Marshal converted to Mobile Church, U.K.

8
Truck, 3 ton, GS, 6×4, Austin K3, U.K.

9
Truck, 30 cwt, GS, 4×2, Chevrolet, converted for Long Range Desert Group, U.K.

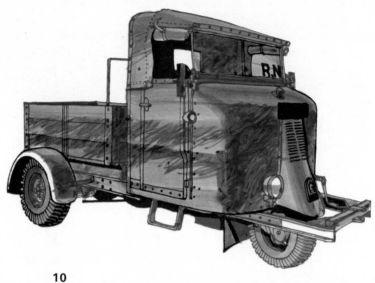

10
Tractor, 3×2, Scammell Mechanical Horse, U.K.

11
Tractor, 3×2, Scammell Mechanical Horse, U.K.

12
Truck, 1½–3 ton, Ordnance Repair, GMC, U.S.A.

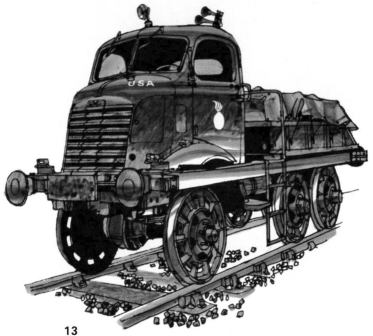

13
Truck, 2½ ton, 6×6, Cargo, GMC, converted to Rail Switcher, U.S.A.

14
Ambulance, 3 ton, 4×2, Bedford ML, U.K.

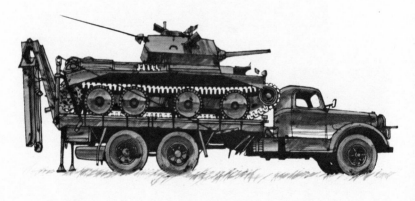

15
Tank Transporter, 18 ton, 6×4, White 920, U.S.A./U.K./France

16
Motor-cycle, solo, Ariel 350 cc, U.K.

17
Car, Light Utility, Austin 10, U.K.

18
Kfz 1 Kubelwagen, Volkswagen 82 (Leichte Personenkraftwagen), Germany

19
Kfz 1/20 Schwimmwagen, Volkswagen 166, Germany

20
Radio Truck, 4×4, Crossley Q, U.K.

21
Lorry, 4×2, 30 cwt, Anti-tank Bedford (armoured), U.K.

22
Truck, 4×2, 4 ton, Fordson Thames, U.K.

23
Bus, AEC Regent, U.K.

24
Car, Light Utility, Standard 12 h.p., U.K.

25
Truck, 8 cwt, FFW, 4×2, Humber, U.K.

26
Motor-cycle Combination, BMW R75, Germany

27
Sfl (Sd Kfz 7/1) with 2 cm Flakvierling, Germany

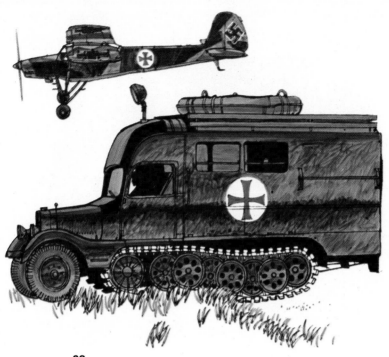

28
Leichte Zugkraftwagen Sd Kfz 11 (Hanomag) converted to
Ambulance, Germany

29
Sfl (Sd Kfz 7/2) with 3·7 cm Flak 36, Germany

30
Ambulance, 1½ ton, 4×2, Chevrolet, U.S.A./U.K.

31
Lorry, Ambulance, Indian Army Type, Australia/India/U.K.

32
Lorry, 3 ton, 6×4, Ford, with Balloon Winch, U.K.

33
Lorry, 30 cwt, GS, 4×2, Dennis, U.K.

34
Light Artillery Tractor, 6×6, Dennis Octolat, U.K.

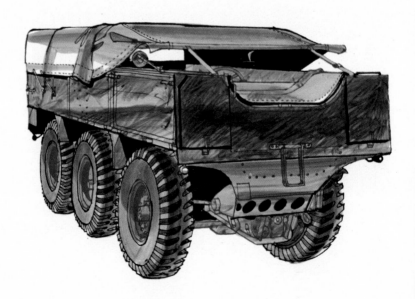

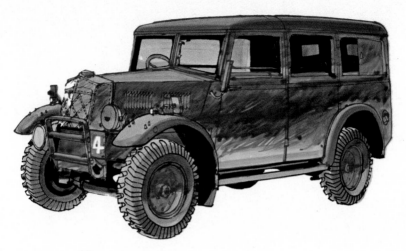

35
Car, Heavy Utility, 4×4, Humber, U.K.

36
Car, Heavy Utility, Ford, U.K.

37
Truck, 15 cwt GS, 4×2, Bedford, U.K.

38
Truck, 15 cwt, Bedford, fitted experimentally with 20 mm Polsten Cannon

39
Lorry, 15 cwt, 4×2, Bedford (Mobile Tea Car), U.K.

40
Lorry, 3 ton, 4×2, Bedford (Stores Van), U.K.

41
Lorry, 3 ton, GS, 4 × 2, Bedford, U.K.

42
Lorry, 3 ton, 4 × 2, Bedford (Bread Van), U.K.

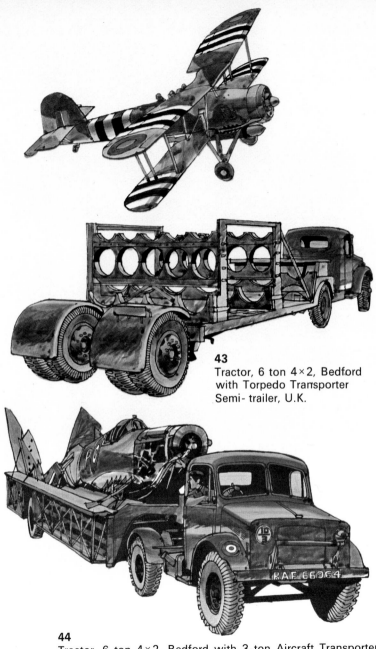

43
Tractor, 6 ton 4×2, Bedford
with Torpedo Transporter
Semi-trailer, U.K.

44
Tractor, 6 ton 4×2, Bedford with 3-ton Aircraft Transporter
Semi-trailer

45
Tractor, 6 ton 4 × 2, Bedford with 3-ton Cargo Semi-trailer, U.K.

46
3 ton Cargo Trailer

47
Lorry, 3 ton, 4×2, 350 gallon Water Carrier, Bedford, U.K.

48
Lorry, 3 ton, 4×4, Fire Tender, Bedford, U.K.

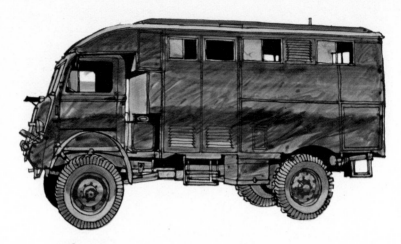

49
Lorry, 3 ton, 4×4, Mobile Laboratory, Bedford, U.K.

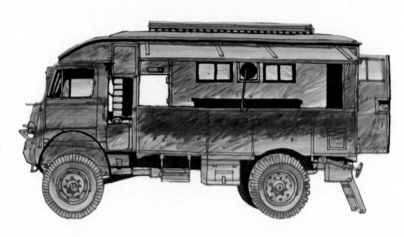

50
Lorry, 3 ton, 4×4, Mobile Canteen, Bedford, U.K.

51
Lorry, 3 ton, 4×4, Command Vehicle, Bedford, U.K.

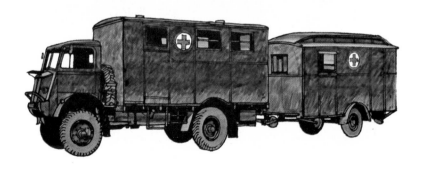

52
Lorry, 3 ton, 4×4, Mobile Dental Surgery, Bedford, U.K.

53
Lorry, 3 ton, 4 × 4, Bedford, experimental (Bedford Giraffe), U.K.

54
Lorry, 3 ton, GS, (Bedford half track), U.K.

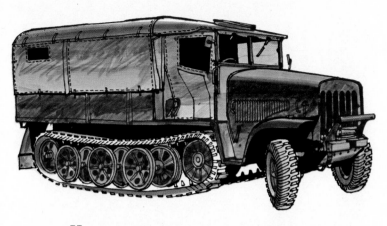

55
Field Artillery Tractor, Bedford Traclat, U.K.

56
Car, Heavy Utility, Ford, Canada/U.K.

57
Mittlerer Gelandegangiger Lastkraftwagen (Opel Blitz, A Type),
Germany

58
Gleisketten-Lkw, 2t, Maultier (Opel Blitz), Germany

59
Mittlerer Personenkraftwagen (Opel Blitz), Germany

60
Schwerer Gelandegangiger Lastkraftwagen (Büssing-NAG),
Germany

61
Schwerer Lastkraftwagen (0) (Tatra 6500/111), Czecho-slovakia/Germany

62
Lorry GS, 15 cwt, 4×2, Dodge, Canada/U.K.

63
Truck, GS, 30 cwt, 4×4, Chevrolet C30, Canada/U.K.

64
Truck, 15 cwt, 4×2, Water Tanker, Chevrolet C15, Canada/U.K.

65
Truck, 8 cwt, 4 × 2, Wireless, Ford F8, Canada/U.K.

66
Truck, 15 cwt, 4 × 4, Chevrolet C15A, Canada/U.K.

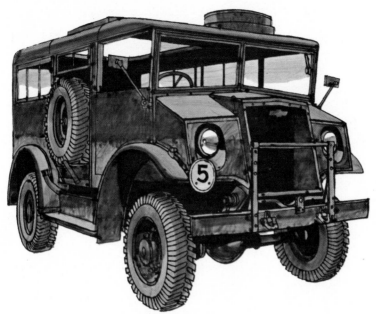

67
Truck, Heavy Utility, 4×4, Chevrolet C8A, Canada/U.K.

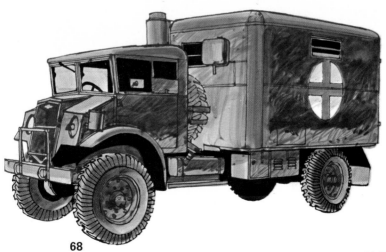

68
Truck, 3 ton, 4×4, Ambulance, Chevrolet C60L, Canada/U.K.

69
Lorry, 15 cwt, Water Contamination, Morris CS8, U.K.

70
Car, Heavy Utility, 4×2, Ford, Canada/U.K.

71
Car, Light Sedan, Ford 21A, U.S.A./Canada/U.K.

72
Car, Heavy Utility, 4×2, Ford, U.S.A./Canada/U.K.

73
Kleine Kettenkraftrad, Sd Kfz 2, Germany

74
Kleine Kettenkraftrad, Sd Kfz 2/1 (Line Layer), Germany

75
Kleine Kettenkraftrad, Sd Kfz 2 (used as gun tractor), Germany

76
Heavy Artillery Tractor, 6×4, Albion CX22, U.K.

77
Tank Transporter and Recovery, 30 ton, Tractor and Semi-trailer, Scammell, U.K.

78
Tractor, Heavy Breakdown, 6×4, Scammell SV/2S, U.K.

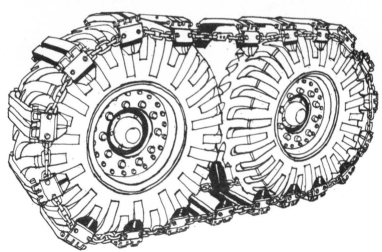

79
W.D. Pattern rubber overall tracks for Scammell Rear Bogie,
U.K.

80
Heavy Artillery Tractor, 6×4, Scammell, R.100, U.K.

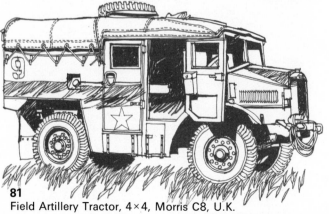

81
Field Artillery Tractor, 4×4, Morris C8, U.K.

82
Tractor, Heavy Breakdown, 6×4, Scammell SV/IT, U.K.

83
Scammell Petrol Bowser, for Bedford 6-ton Prime Mover, U.K.

84
Truck, 2½ ton, 6×4, Cargo, Studebaker, U.S.A.

85
Truck, 2½ ton, 6×4, Cargo, GMC, U.S.A.

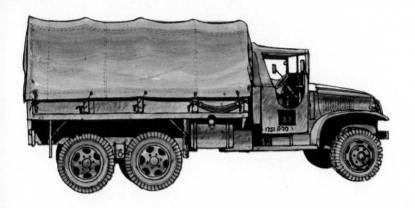

86
Truck, 2½ ton, 6×4, Cargo, GMC, U.S.A.

87
Truck, 2½ ton, 6×6, Cargo, Dump, GMC, U.S.A.

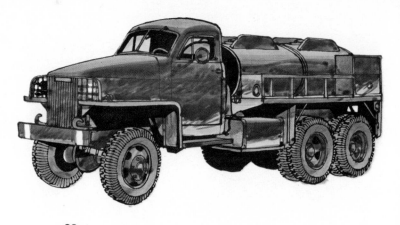

88
Truck, 2½ ton, 6×6, Gasoline Tank, Studebaker, U.S.A.

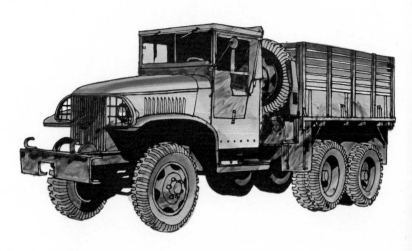

89
Truck, 2½ ton, 6×6, Cargo, GMC, U.S.A.

90
Truck, ½ ton, 4×4, Ambulance, Dodge, U.S.A.

91
Truck, 6 ton, 4×4, Cargo, FWD, U.S.A.

92
Truck, 2½ ton, 6×6, GMC, COE Type, U.S.A.

93
Truck, 4–5 ton, 4×4, Federal with 10-ton Refrigerated Trailer, U.S.A.

94
Bus, 2½ ton, 4×2, International K7, U.S.A.

95
M2 High-speed Tractor, 7 ton, Cletrac M2, U.S.A.

96
Truck, 1½ ton, 4×4, Bomb Service Vehicle, U.S.A.

97
Bomb Handling Trolley, U.S.A.

98
M20 Prime Mover, Truck, 12 ton, 6×4, Diamond T, U.S.A./U.K.

99
M9 Trailer, 40 tons. British Mark I, U.K.

100
Autocarro Unificato Medio, 5 ton, 4×2, Fiat 665, Italy

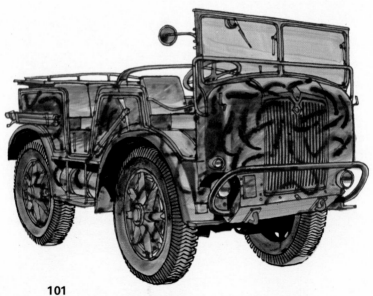

101
Trattore Medio, 4×4, Fiat TM40, Italy/Germany

102
M2 Truck-mounted Crane (Thew Shovell MC 6×6) and
M16 3-ton Trailer, U.S.A.

103
M26 Truck-Tractor, 12 ton, 6×6, with M15 Tank Transporter
Semi-trailer, U.S.A.

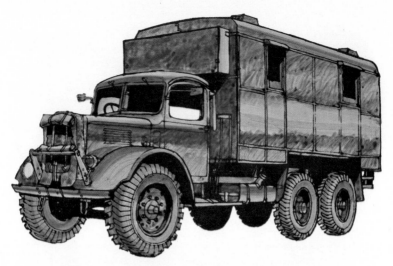

104
Lorry, 3 ton, 6×4, Signals Office, Austin K6, U.K.

105
Lorry, 3 ton, 6×4, Breakdown Gantry, Austin K6, U.K.

106
Lorry, 3 ton, GS, 4×4, Austin K5, U.K.

107
Lorry, 4×4, Anti-Tank Portee (6 pdr.), Austin K5, U.K.

109
Truck, $\frac{1}{4}$ ton, 4×4, Command Reconnaissance, Willys MA, U.S.A.

108
Truck, $\frac{1}{4}$ ton, 4×4, Command Reconnaissance, Ford GPW in
British Service as Royal Signals Line Layer, U.S.A./U.K.

110
Truck, $\frac{1}{4}$ ton, 4×4, Utility, Willys MB, with 3-litter Ambulance
Kit, U.S.A./U.K.

111
Truck, $\frac{1}{4}$ ton, 4×4, Utility, Ford GPW, converted for 'Jeep Railway', U.S.A./U.K.

112
Truck, $\frac{1}{4}$ ton, 4×4, Amphibian, Ford GPA, U.S.A.

113
Lorry, 3 ton, 4×4, Breakdown Gantry, Ford WOT6, U.K.

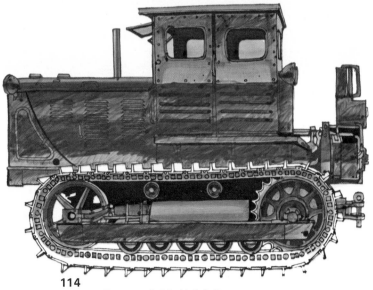

114
Artillery Tractor, S-80, U.S.S.R.

115
Lorry, 3 ton, 4×2, Petrol carrier, Dennis, U.K.

116
Lorry, 3 ton, 4×2, Tipping, Dennis, U.K.

117
M5, 13 ton, High-speed Tractor, U.S.A.

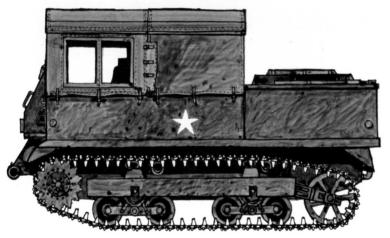

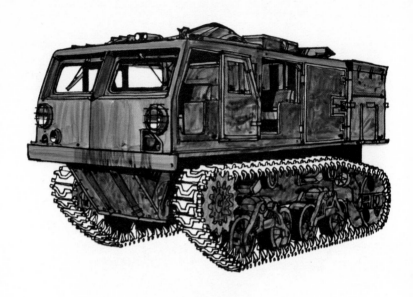

118
M4, 18 ton, High-speed Tractor, U.S.A.

119
M6, 38 ton, High-speed Tractor, U.S.A.

120
Truck, ¾ ton, 4×4, Command Car, Dodge, U.S.A.

121
Truck, ¾ ton, 4×4, Command Reconnaissance Car, Dodge, U.S.A.

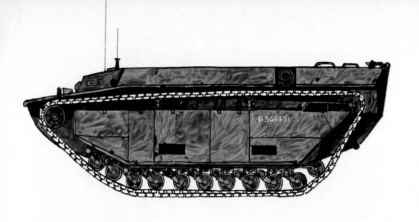

122
Landing Vehicle Tracked, Armoured, Mk 4—LVT4, U.S.A./U.K.

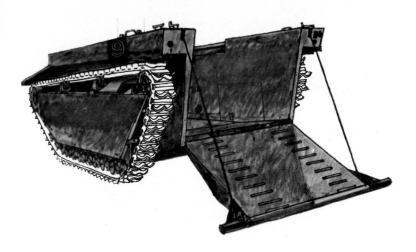

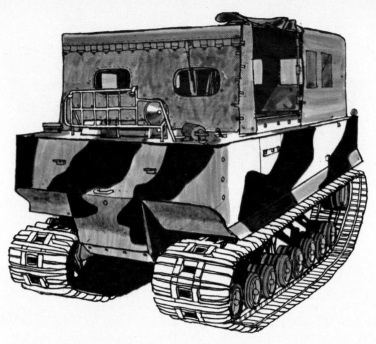

123
M29 Cargo Carrier, Weasel, U.S.A./U.K.

124
M29C Cargo Carrier, Amphibious, Weasel, U.S.A./U.K.

125
Kfz 31 Krankenkraftwagen (4×4, Phänomen Granit 1500A),
Germany

126
Schwerer Personenkraftwagen (4×4, Phänomen Granit 1500A),
Germany

127
Truck, Amphibious, 2½ ton, 6×6, DUKW, U.S.A./U.K.

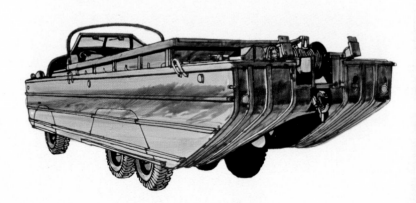

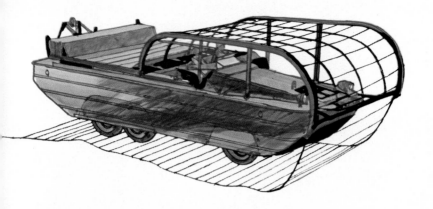

128
Truck, Amphibious, 2½ ton, 6×6, DUKW with Experimental
Mat-laying Equipment, U.S.A.

129
Schwerer Gelandegangiger Lastkraftwagen offen (4×4
Mercedes Benz L4500A, A Type), Germany

130
GAZ-67B Field Car, U.S.S.R.

131
Ostradschlepper (4×4, Skoda 175), Germany

132
Raupenschlepper-Ost (Steyr RSO/01), Germany

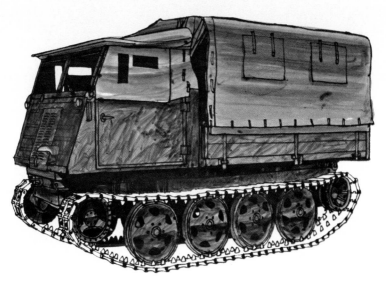

133
Raupenschlepper-Ost (Steyr RSO/03), Germany

134
Tractor, 20 ton, 6×6, Scammell Constructor, U.K.

136
Truck, 4×4, 10 ton Scammell Mountaineer, U.K.

135
Dozer on 20-ton Low-loading Machinery Trailer, U.K.

137
Tractor, 10 ton, 6×6, GS Recovery, Scammell, U.K.

138
Truck, 7½ ton, 6×6, Prime Mover, Mack NO, U.S.A.

139
Truck, ¾ ton, 4×4, Weapons Carrier, Dodge, U.S.A.

140
Truck, 4 ton, 6×6, Van, Diamond T, U.S.A.

141
Truck, 4 ton, 6×6, Dumper, Diamond T, U.S.A.

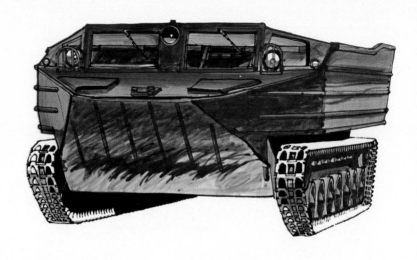

142
Amphibious Personnel Carrier K-61, U.S.S.R.

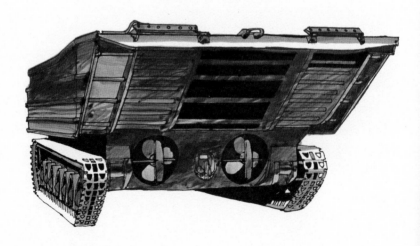

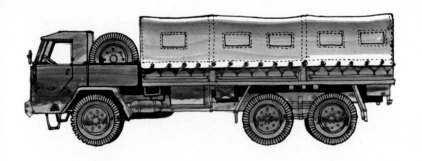

143
LKW, 10 ton, 6×6, Faun 908/54VA, Federal Germany

144
LKW, 10 ton, 6×6, Faun L912/21 HOH, Federal Germany

145
LKW, 12 ton, 6×6, Faun L912/54A, Federal Germany

146
Truck, 10 ton, 6×6, Bridging Crane, AEC Militant, U.K.

147
Light Wheeled Loader, Michigan, U.S.A./U.K.

148
Articulated Wheel Loader, Allis-Chalmers 645, U.K.

149
Tractor, Wheeled, 10 ton, GS, 6×6, Medium Artillery, Leyland, U.K.

150
Tractor, 10 ton, Leyland with Bofors Light AA gun, U.K.

151
Truck, GS, $\frac{1}{4}$ ton, 4×4, Rover 8 (Land Rover) with M40A1
106 mm Recoiless Rifle, U.K.

152
Truck, GS, $\frac{3}{4}$ ton, 4×4 Rover 9 (Land Rover) with Wombat
Anti-tank Gun, U.K.

153
Truck, GS, Utility $\frac{1}{2}$ ton, 4×4, Land Rover, U.K.

154
Ambulance, 2—4 stretcher, $\frac{3}{4}$ ton, 4×4 (Rover 9), U.K.

155
Truck, Fire Fighting, $\frac{3}{4}$ ton, 4×4, Land Rover, U.K.

156
Truck, Cab Forward, Fire Fighting, 1 ton, 4×4, Forward control, Land Rover, U.K.

157
Truck, GS, $\frac{3}{4}$ ton, with Rapier Ground-to-air Missile Launching Fire and Power Unit, U.K.

158
Rapier Missile, Fire, Power, and Tracking Units, U.K.

159
Truck, 4×4, $\frac{1}{2}$ ton, GS, Lightweight Air Portable, Land Rover, U.K.

160
Truck Cargo, 1 ton, 4×4, Land Rover, Forward Control, U.K.

161
Car, Light, 4×2 Morris 1000 Traveller, U.K.

162
Car, Medium, 4×2, Austin 1800, U.K.

163
Car, Medium, 4×2, Ford Zephyr, U.K.

165
Tractor, Wheeled, 6×6, 20 ton, Scammell Contractor with
50—60 ton Semi-trailer Tank Transporter, Crane-Fruehauf, U.K.

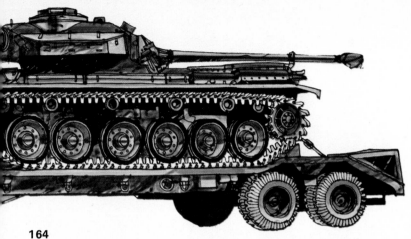

164
Tractor, Wheeled, 6×6, 20 ton, Scammell Super Constructor
with 50—60 ton Semi-trailer Tank Transporter, Crane-
Fruehauf, U.K.

166
Tractor, Wheeled, 6×6, 20 ton, Scammell Super Constructor
with Ballast Body, U.K.

167
Tractor, Heavy Recovery, 6×6, Scammell Super 90 Constructor,
U.K.

168
Tractor, Wheeled, 6×6, 20 ton, Scammell Contractor with ballast body

169
Airfield Fire Tender, 6×6, Thornycroft Nubian Mk VII, U.K.

170
Truck, Cargo, 4×4, 3 ton, Bedford RL, U.K.

171
Thunderbird, High-level Air Defence Missile, U.K.

172
Truck, Cargo, 4×4, Air Portable, Dropside Bedford RL, with
3-ton Transportable Container, U.K.

173
Truck-mounted Repair Shop, 4×4, 3 ton, Bedford RL, U.K.

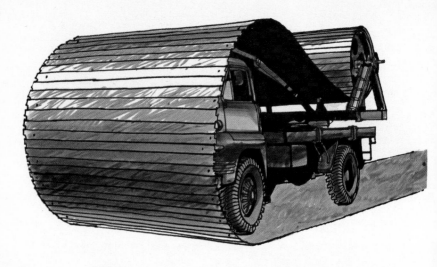

174
Class 30 Trackway (portable roadway) mounted on Truck,
Cargo, Dropside, 4×4, 3 ton, Bedford RL, U.K.

175
Rough Terrain Fork Lift Tractor, Eager Beaver, U.K.

176
Tracked Carrier, Volvo BV 200, Sweden/U.K.

177
Tractor, Wheeled, GS, 20 ton, 6×6, Scammell, U.K.

178
Truck, 5 ton, Cargo, High Mobility Load Carrier, 6×6, Alvis
Stalwart Mk 2, U.K.

DESCRIPTIVE NOTES

1 **Field Artillery Tractor, 4 × 4, Morris C8,** 1940–44, U.K.

Earliest of the British Army's range of fully-enclosed field artillery tractors was the Guy Quad Ant, which appeared in 1938 as a towing vehicle for the 18-pdr. field gun. (This particular vehicle is described in the previous volume in this series). These enclosed vehicles were a major advance on previous types of artillery tractor, having fittings and layout specially designed for their artillery role. Comfortable weather-protected seating was provided for the six-man crew of the gun detachment (driver, gun commander, and four gun numbers) and there was storage for ammunition and battery stores in the rear compartment. There was an opening roof hatch above the front passenger seat, and a bracket on the sloping rear body plate to take either a spare wheel or the gun traversing platform. The vehicle towed a limber (containing ammunition) and the field gun which was initially an 18-pdr., a weapon replaced by the well-known 25-pdr. gun-howitzer from 1940.

By 1939 field artillery tractors were being produced by Morris as well as Guy and the Morris version (designated C8 by Morris-Commercial Cars Ltd) became one of the best-known and most familiar of all British military types.

This vehicle had a four-wheel-drive chassis which featured a 4-ton winch driven from the transfer gearbox and able to be led forward or to the rear. In the original model the vehicle could only be driven through all four wheels. Later models, however, had provision for dis-engaging to two-wheel drive in all gears except first. The engine was the standard four-cylinder petrol unit also used in other contemporary Morris types.

Despite this vehicle's replacement in production from 1944 by an improved (Mk V) version, the original type of tractor remained in British Army use until at least 1954 and even in 1970 it was possible to see vehicles of this type in commercial or public service (as snow-ploughs or light recovery trucks).

The Morris C8 field artillery tractor was 14 ft 8¾ in. long, 7¼ ft wide, and 7 ft 5 in. high. The empty weight was 3 tons 7 cwt. This vehicle was popularly known as the 'Quad' Canadian Ford, and Chevrolet vehicles were also turned out as field artillery tractors with similar bodywork.

2 **Field Artillery Tractor, 4 × 4, Ford (Canadian Military Pattern),** 1941–45, Canada/U.K.

As stated above, the field artillery tractors, built in Canada from 1941 onwards for British and Commonwealth use had an enclosed body based on the British WD pattern, first introduced in the Guy 'Quad Ant' (plate 156, previous volume in this series) and the Morris C8 (Plate 1, above). The Canadian-built vehicles were based on Ford and Chevrolet chassis. Over the years several production changes took place in line with those introduced on the British vehicles. The FAT-1 had a fully enclosed roof with only a hatch over the front passenger seat as shown in the Morris C8 illustration (Plate 1). Apart from the bonnet shape it was externally similar to the Morris. The

FAT-2 had a large open section in the roof with a canvas cover plus two small rear view windows, again in similar style to the later production Morris C8. The FAT-3 had the entire rear sloping roof open with a canvas cover, and introduced the new standard No. 13 cab with distinctive sloped forward windscreen (for mpre details see under Plate 66). The FAT-4 had a spare wheel on the rear roof in place of the traversing platform formerly carried here. The centre roof section was open and provided with a canvas cover. The FAT-5 was similar but fully winterised for sub-zero temperatures. The FAT-6, last type produced, had an open body with canvas cover similar to the late production Morris C8 FAT (Plate 81).

All these vehicles were winch-fitted, were 14 ft 7 in. or 9 in. long, and 7½ ft wide. They had a Mercury V8 engine in the case of the Ford model or a six-cylinder GMC engine in the case of the externally similar Chevrolet models.

3   **Medium Artillery Tractor, 4 × 4, AEC Matador**
4   **Medium Artillery Tractor, 4 × 4, AEC Matador with 5·5 in. gun-howitzer,** 1939–45, U.K.

The Matador was the longest-lived of the gun tractors produced by Britain in World War II and scores of these famous vehicles were still to be seen in 1970 serving in a civilian capacity as maids-of-all-work for civil engineering contractors and service stations. Some others still remained in service use in 1970, being then up to 30 years old and as good as new. The Matador tractor first appeared early in 1939 and met a War Office specification for medium gun

tractors which provided seating for the gun crew and ready-use ammunition stowage in the truck-type body. These vehicles hauled the 6 in. 4·5 in., or 5·5 in. howitzer (Plate 4) and later (post-war mainly) were used to pull the 3·7 in. AA gun and its associated generator and radar trailers. Early vehicles had a steel cab roof, later replaced by a canvas roof, with either a canvas covered hatch or a circular metal-framed hatchway. The body had side doors, steps, and a canvas tilt with roll-up sides. Shell carriers were attached to runners on the body floor to facilitate sliding the rounds up to the tailgate when the gun was emplaced for action. On early vehicles (Plate 3) a small platform in front of the windscreen carried a gas-detector patch but this was later discarded.

The Matador had a six-cylinder 7·58 litre AEC engine of 95 b.h.p. This gave a top speed of about 36 m.p.h. A 7-ton winch with 250 ft of wire rope was mounted inside the chassis members with pull to the front or rear. The vehicle could tow up to 6½ tons. Plate 4 shows a Matador in Italy in 1943 displaying the then current British air recognition marking of a red-white-blue roundel similar to the RAF aircraft marking. Total production of Matadors for the British army reached 8,612. The other major Matador user was the Royal Air Force whose 400 vehicles were in either load carrier (steel dropside body), flatbed, or mobile airfield control forms. The latter had a box-type office body. Some Matadors remained in RAF service as late as 1970. Further variations on the chassis included armoured command, and armoured demolition vehicles, while there was also an experimental version with half-tracks. The Matador was 20 ft

9 in. long, 10 ft 2 in. high, and 7 ft 10½ in. wide.

5 and 6 Flight Refueller, 2,500 gallons, 6 × 6, AEC 0854, 1941, U.K.

This vehicle was principally used by the Royal Air Force as a high capacity fuel bowser. Though superficially it resembled the Matador, it was, in fact, based on the chassis of the AEC Marshal (Plate 134, previous volume in this series) which was introduced in the 1930s. Cab, transmission and wheels were, however, all taken from the Matador. The vehicle had a six-cylinder diesel engine giving 95 b.h.p. It was the largest fuelling vehicle in RAF service and was mainly used on bomber stations. The drawings show the opening rear doors giving access to the pump controls and a folding rear ladder.

Another widely used vehicle built on this chassis was the Coles VII Mobile Crane which was also used by the RAF for aircraft recovery and handling. This had a 360° slewing 5-ton Coles crane mounted on a turntable towards the rear of the chassis frame. In this case a separate Ford V8 engine was carried within the crane housing to provide a power source for operating.

7 Truck, 3 ton, GS, 6 × 4, AEC Marshal converted to Mobile Church, 1942, U.K.

Shown here is a most unusual local modification which was carried out by a Royal Army Ordnance Corps workshop in the North African desert in the 1941–42 period. This was the 'Motor Church of St. George' and started life as an AEC Marshal Bridging Vehicle, illustrated in its original form in Plate 135 of the previous volume. This was a redundant vehicle which had its bridge cradles removed to leave the bare chassis. A wooden caravan type structure was built on and suitably decorated. The doors at the rear opened to reveal an altar, and church services were usually held in the open air. The rest of the structure formed an office and quarters for the padre who drove himself around from unit to unit.

8 Truck, 3 ton, GS, 6 × 4, Austin K3, 1939, U.K.

Development of the ubiquitous British 6 × 4 3-ton military truck was described in detail in the previous volume. By 1939 plans were in hand to replace the 6 × 4 3-ton type by a new 4 × 4 3-ton type. However, production of four-wheel drive types did not start until early 1941, so the 6 × 4 type remained in wide use during the early war years. Most of the types in production prior to the outbreak of war remained in service throughout the whole 1939–45 period, and many of them stayed in production as well. Vehicles in this category were made by AEC, Albion, Thornycroft, Crossley, Karrier, Ford, and Leyland. A typical 1939 production vehicle was the Austin K3/YF which followed the standard GS layout with well-type body, WD patent articulated rear bogie, and folding canvas top and side screens. The bonnet was the contemporary type used in Austin commercial vehicles of the same period.

A comparison with early 6 × 4 3-ton types such as the Karrier and Crossley (Plates 105 and 106, previous volume) shows how little the basic layout changed between 1926 and 1939.

Even after 4 × 4 types started to be produced later on, the 6 × 4 type remained in wide service, in particular for auxiliary roles for which special bodies were too long to fit the new 4 × 4 chassis. Austin 6 × 4 vehicles remained in production throughout the war. The K3 was replaced in production by the K6 from 1944, a vehicle which was basically similar to the K3 but which had a modified version of the Austin commercial cab and a simplified bonnet. The K3 truck was 21 ft 11 in. long, 7½ ft wide, and 10 ft 4½ in. high. It has a six-cylinder, 72 b.h.p. engine.

9 Truck, 30 cwt, GS, 4 × 2, Chevrolet, converted for Long Range Desert Group, 1941, U.K.

In June 1940 the war spread to North Africa when Italy declared war on Britain and eventually made threatening movements from Libya against the Egyptian border which was patrolled by British forces. The value of motor transport for policing and patrolling vast tracts of desert had been amply demonstrated by the Light Car Patrols of the First World War, which had operated in the Western Desert, Mesopotamia and Palestine. Their exploits are described in the previous book in this series. In the 1920s several French and British private expeditions had crossed the North African desert, one led by R. A. Bagnold, a keen explorer whose subsequent work included a study of the physical characteristics of desert topography. He also perfected a means of desert navigation based on star and sun sights, similar in style to marine navigation. When the

Italians declared war in 1940 and seemed likely to invade Egypt, British forces were thinly distributed to guard the country and were greatly outnumbered by the Italians. Bagnold, who lived in Egypt, had joined the army and lost no time in suggesting to General Wavell, the British commander in Egypt, that armed motorised reconnaissance patrols would be a simple means of patrolling and protecting the inland flanks of the frontier with minimum manpower. The Italians were well mechanised and there was a possibility that they would make motorised forays into Egypt.

General Wavell was most receptive to Bagnold's ideas; he had already employed motorised raiding parties in peacetime manoeuvres some years previously and he now put Bagnold in charge of the desert patrol project. The patrol force was organised at top speed and Bagnold recruited crews from friends with desert driving experience, and volunteers from both New Zealand and British units. The vehicles used had to be rugged and capacious enough to carry stores for long journeys. Bagnold selected the Chevrolet 30-cwt truck which was then being delivered to the Egyptian Army. Some 15-cwt Chevrolet trucks were also acquired, though the drawing depicts the 30-cwt version. Both these types of truck were based on the 1939 Canadian Chevrolet chassis and bonnet but they had military GS bodies. The 30-cwt was built in Canada and exported while the 15-cwt models were assembled in India from Canadian parts.

To suit the vehicles to the rigours of desert patrol work, Bagnold had them extensively modified, incorporating changes suggested by his peacetime experience on desert expeditions. Cab tops and side doors were removed, condensers were fitted to the radiators to conserve cooling water, sand channels and canvas sand mats were carried, pintles were fitted to take machine guns, leaf springs were strengthened, and 'balloon' tyres replaced the normal tyres. Two tons of stores, ammunition and demolition equipment were carried in the back and vehicles usually had a crew of four men. By late August 1940 the first patrol made its first sortie to reconnoitre the southern flank of the Egypt-Libya border. Subsequently, the Long Range Desert Group (LRDG) as it was called made a series of now legendary patrols into the Western Desert, well behind the front line, watching, waiting and reporting on enemy moves. On some occasions the patrols also made sabotage and raiding missions but these activities were secondary to the main one which was gathering and sending information on enemy troop movements. A patrol could last for many weeks under the desert sun and there were many deeds of great heroism by individuals among the crews. Patrols usually consisted of four trucks. The navigator's vehicle carried a sun-compass on its dashboard. LRDG operations continued on a big scale (with increasing manpower and more patrols) until late 1942 when this unique unit was disbanded with the cessation of the desert fighting. The pink colour scheme shown was chosen to blend into the pinkish desert sand.

The basic Chevrolet truck had a 85 h.p. six-cylinder engine and a 134 in. wheelbase. Aside from the basic truck, the 30-cwt Chevrolet was also produced in ambulance and water tanker forms and the type was widely used in the Middle East.

10 and 11   Tractor, 3 × 2, Scammell Mechanical Horse, 1940, U.K.

The Scammell MH6 Mechanical Horse was basically a commercial type of vehicle, much used by British railway companies for parcels delivery work. The original design appeared in about 1930, and it was intended, as its name implies, as a replacement for the horse in commercial cartage service. The early models had an attachment whereby the front turntable of a horse-drawn dray could be attached for towing. Subsequently rubber-tyred semi-trailers were provided. Mechanical Horses were purchased in some numbers by the British services in 1939–40 and were mainly used in store and supply yards, dockyards, and air bases, for general cargo and store handling. Most service vehicles had a ballast body and towed trains of light four-wheel trailers (lower picture) which could be left as required alongside rail wagons or heavy trucks for transhipment. There were several variations on the basic design. The top drawing shows a Royal Navy vehicle with soft canvas cab top and front tow bar, while the lower drawing shows a Royal Army Service Corps vehicle with the more usual hardtop cab. Interestingly enough this little-known service type was also one of the longest lived. They were still in use by the British Army as late as 1967–68 long after they had disappeared from commercial use in favour of later designs. The Mechanical Horse had a cab-mounted 36 h.p. engine and its wheelbase was 9 ft 2½ in.

12   Truck, 1½–3 ton, Ordnance Repair, GMC, 1940, U.S.A.

The U.S. Army Quartermaster Corps

were responsible for military transport in the American Army prior to July 1942. In the 1920s and 1930s they made creditable efforts—within the severe limitations of the defence budgets of the time—to prepare for further expansion and to standardise military transport types and requirements since the standard truck programme of the 1917–19 period—the 'Liberty' trucks—had proved something of a fiasco (as recounted in the previous volume). In fact, it proved impossible for both political and financial reasons to evolve standard military designs, but some specific requirements for the future were formulated. In September 1939, when the war in Europe started it was decided to speed up procurement of the vastly increased number of trucks needed by standardising on five classes of chassis—$\frac{1}{2}$-ton, $1\frac{1}{2}$-ton, $2\frac{1}{2}$-ton, 4-ton and $7\frac{1}{2}$-ton. The trucks themselves, though, were to be ordinary commercial types with such minimal alterations as were needed to suit them for military use. A typical military requirement was for four-wheel-drive for vehicles in certain roles, one of which was ordnance repair or maintenance where trucks frequently had to operate in or near front line conditions. FWD four-wheel-drive vehicles had been similarly used for this role in 1917–19 with great success. In the $1\frac{1}{2}$-ton class no suitable four-wheel-drive chassis was available so normal 4 × 2 GMC (General Motors Corporation) 4 × 2 trucks were used instead, specially converted to 4 × 4 configuration by the addition of a power transfer gearbox and live front axle. The chassis and cab remained the normal commercial type but military additions included army pattern towing pintle,

metal stone guard at the front, and heavy duty tyres. The chassis was known as a COE type (cab-over engine) a layout known as 'forward control' in Britain. This $1\frac{1}{2}$-ton 4 × 4 type came into wide service in 1940 with the massive expansion of the U.S. Army.

The ordnance repair truck shown carried work bench and tools and the lower side panels dropped to form a working platform. The upper side panels were raised to form an awning. The body structure featured plywood and light metal sheeting. Other types on this same chassis included an air compressor unit, cargo body and ordnance maintenance vehicles with integral van-type bodies. The ordnance maintenance trucks were supplied with different tool equipment and internal layouts for a variety of different specialist tasks including small arms repair, instrument repair, automotive repair, tank maintenance, welding, machining, and so on. Some of these types were subsequently provided to the British and other Allied armies. From early 1942 onwards, these COE vehicles were replaced by similar types on the $2\frac{1}{2}$-ton GMC normal control chassis. After this the ordnance repair trucks of the type shown were stripped of their internal fittings and were used as cargo carriers.

In addition to the 4 × 4 conversion described and shown here, the GMC, COE $1\frac{1}{2}$-ton type was also used in its original 4 × 2 form, mainly with an integral panel van type body fitted as a signal truck with windows and side doors.

This GMC vehicle had a 100-h.p., six-cylinder engine, a 13 in. wheelbase, and an overall length of 218 in.

13 Truck, 2½ ton, 6 × 6, Cargo, GMC, converted to Rail Switcher, 1943, U.S.A.

The 2½-ton 6 × 6 COE type was virtually a three-axle version of the 1½-ton model shown in Plate 12. Again it was based on the commercial GMC cab and chassis 6 × 4 model, and was converted by the manufacturers to 6 × 6 type by the addition of a transfer box and live front axle. Unlike the 1½-ton model, however, this 2½-tonner remained in production and service until the war ended. It was built by the Yellow Truck and Coach Mfg. Co., a subsidiary of General Motors. The cargo truck model had a steel body and this was produced in both short and long body forms. The short (15 ft) body had folding slatted bench seats for secondary use as a troop carrier. The long (17 ft) body was cargo only. Illustrated here is a local modification of the short-bodied version with its wheels replaced by flanged railway wheels and scrap iron ballast weights in the body section. A number of vehicles were so converted to act as switchers (shunters) at U.S. Ordnance Corps railheads in Europe in 1944–45. The Ordnance Corps badge can be seen on the cab doors. Buffing plates and support girders were added, plus an access ladder to the cab.

During 1942 there was a production change when the pressed steel cab was eliminated and replaced by a canvas roof and side sheets. The appearance was then similar to the COE type shown in Plate 92. This GMC COE type was widely used throughout the war. Some vehicles were refitted with short steel tipping dumper bodies for Engineers Corps use. This vehicle had a 104-b.h.p., six-cylinder engine and a 164 in. wheelbase. It was 24 ft 1½ in. long with 17 ft cargo body. The dump truck versions had their wheelbase reduced by about 40 in.

14 Ambulance, 3 ton, 4 × 2, Bedford ML, 1940–45, U.K.

The standard British heavy military ambulance used throughout World War II and well into the 1950s (and even the 1960s in a few cases) featured a large, box-like wood and fabric body built by Mann Egerton, the well-known coachbuilding firm. Shutter and mushroom type ventilators were incorporated and there were twin rear doors, though some vehicles had only a canvas screen. The major chassis used for this ambulance was the Austin K2 of which over 13,000 were built. This had a similar front end to the Austin 3-tonner shown in Plate 8. The next most widely used chassis was the Bedford ML, shown here, which was superficially very similar to the Austin except for the Bedford commercial-type bonnet which had extra side vents for improved cooling. The chassis was based on the normal Bedford 30 cwt commercial chassis and, in fact, the British Army also used the ordinary Bedford lorry on the same chassis. The same ambulance body was also used on a Morris-Commercial chassis. The Bedford was 19 ft long, 9 ft 2 in. high and 7 ft 3 in. wide. It had a 72 b.h.p. engine. This type of ambulance could carry 4 stretchers, two each side, or 10 seated wounded. It was a widely-used type which saw service on all fronts and was also supplied to most of the Allied nations, including America. Some vehicles of this type were used by the Civil Defence organisation in Great Britain as well.

15 Tank Transporter, 18 ton, 6 × 4, White 920, 1940, U.S.A./U.K./France

In France the idea had evolved during World War I of carrying tanks on trucks to the battle zone, thereby conserving the tracks and motors to the last minute before going into action. This was mainly due to the inherent mechanical unreliability of the early tanks. The Americans, who used French tanks in 1918, followed the same practice. After 1918 both the new French and new American tank-building programmes called for tanks with limits (5 tons— light; 15 tons—medium) which allowed them to be carried on trucks. The White 920 was one of several American heavy commercial types of truck suitable for carrying tanks of up to about 15 tons in weight, and vehicles of this type were ordered by France in 1939. By the time delivery was due in 1940, however, France had been overrun and the British Army took them over. With modifications to the bodies and ramps they were put into service in Britain and in the Western Desert. These vehicles could carry the heaviest cruiser tanks then in British service, such as the A13 (Cruiser Tank Mk I) as shown in the drawing. With much bigger tanks coming into service, however, these vehicles went out of use as tank transporters. The folding ramps were wound up and down by hand winches. The White 920 was 29 ft 10 in. long and 10¼ ft wide. Empty weight was 11 tons 4 cwt.

16 Motor cycle, solo, Ariel 350 cc, 1940–42, U.K.

The motor cycle was widely used by all forces in World War II. Typical of many solo types of machine used by the British was the 350 cc Ariel, a conventional type with O.H.V. engine and girder forks. It was based on the ordinary commercial Ariel type with no special changes for military service. The drawing shows a despatch rider of the 1st Armoured Division in early 1941 wearing a protective anti-gas suit, and anti-gas respirator. Note how the mapboard opens, also the position of the famous 1st Armoured Division horned rhinocerous emblem on the fuel tank.

This vehicle was 7 ft long and its 350 cc single-cylinder engine gave 12½ b.h.p.

17 Car, Light Utility, Austin 10, 1940–45, U.K.

This light vehicle with what is now called a 'pick-up' truck body was used extensively by British and Allied forces from 1940 onwards, mainly in Europe. In the early days of the war they were also used by fighting units, but later they were more restricted to home, base, or depot service since the American Jeep (Plate 108) took over the function of the light utility car in field units. The vehicle shown was based on the 1939 Austin 10 car and had a bonnet (except for three side louvres) and cab identical to the car. The spare wheel was mounted in a recess on the cab roof and there was a removable canvas tilt over the load space. Rootes (Hillman), Morris, and Standard all made similar vehicles based on their respective 10 or 12 h.p. car equivalents. The Navy and RAF also used these vehicles. The wheelbase of the Austin 10 Light Utility was 7 ft 10¾ in., and it was 13 ft long. Typical employment was in signals, military police, or divisional HQ units.

18 Kfz 1 Kubelwagen, Volkswagen 82 (Leichte Personenkraftwagen), 1940–45, Germany

The Volkswagen Type 82 was a military derivation of the Volkswagen 'People's Car' which dated back in conception to 1933 when Hitler asked the noted automobile engineer Dr. Ferdinand Porsche to design a simple and inexpensive car which would put motoring within the financial reach of all. Early in 1934 Porsche completed detailed specifications for approval and was given the go-ahead to make prototypes and two pre-production batches of 30 cars each for testing and demonstration. The vehicle was to have a 996-cc rear-mounted air-cooled engine and was to be sold at DM 1,000. A new factory was to be built at Wolfsburg to produce the new car in quantity. The Volkswagen was a small streamlined sedan and four decades later the developed version of this same basic design remains familiar all over the world as the Volkswagen 'Beetle', one of the best-selling cars of all time. The Volkswagen car did not, in fact, enter production until after 1945, however, for in 1939 Germany marched into Czechoslovakia and war became inevitable. Porsche was asked to design immediately a militarised version of the Volkswagen for the German Army which was still, at this time, less than adequately equipped with motor transport despite the efficiency of its armoured divisions. The military Volkswagen was based closely on the car, utilising the same rear engine, chassis pan, wheels and suspension. The sedan type body was, however, completely replaced with a simplified box-like open structure reduced entirely to flat panels for ease of

production and assembly. The design was ready for approval in December 1939 and some prototypes were sent to Poland for 'field trials' by Panzer divisions. Here the vehicles were favourably received being easy to handle and having an excellent cross-country performance. Some ordnance officers had earlier feared that the small rear-mounted engine and lack of four-wheel-drive would render the vehicle unsuitable for military use. They were proved wrong, however, and the Volkswagen Kubelwagen became the most widely used and best-known German vehicle of the war period. By May 1945 no less than 52,018 Volkswagens had been built and they were used by all arms of the Wehrmacht including the Navy and Luftwaffe. Production actually started in March 1940 and a few vehicles were in service in time for the invasion of France and Flanders. General Rommel was, at this time, a divisional general but when he went to take command of the Afrika Korps in 1941 he realised that Volkswagens would be ideal for use in the desert. Here whole reconnaissance battalions were equipped with Kubelwagens and the vehicle more than justified its existence. The major demand for Kubelwagens was on the Eastern Front, however, after Germany had invaded Russia in mid 1941. Here the extremes of climate proved as big an enemy as the Red Army at times, and mud and snow proved major obstacles to troop movements in the winter months. The Kubelwagen was one of the few motor vehicles which proved to be 'at home' in these conditions; its very light weight ($\frac{1}{2}$ ton) prevented bogging down and it could be manhandled by two men. The Kubelwagen (officially Leichte Personenkraftwagen—light personal carrier) was used by all branches of the Army and Waffen—SS. Roles included staff car, light ambulance, ammunition carrier, and assault engineer carrier. The latter involved the addition of an extra stores locker in the right hand rear seat. The Kubelwagen was $12\frac{1}{4}$ ft long, $5\frac{1}{4}$ ft wide, $5\frac{1}{2}$ ft high (with the canvas tilt raised) and had a 7 ft 11 in. wheelbase. It weighed 1,470 lbs and had a 985-cc rear-mounted air-cooled engine. Later vehicles (from 1943) had a 1,131-cc engine and smaller headlights.

19 Kfz 1/20 Schwimmwagen, Volkswagen 166, 1942–44, Germany

Popularly called the Schwimmwagen but officially known as a Schwimmfahiger, this was an amphibious version of the standard Volkswagen Type 82. This vehicle was mechanically similar to the Type 82 but had a bath-shaped pressed steel body with a three-bladed propeller on a lifting rear arm. Dr. Porsche designed the Schwimmwagen specifically for the wet conditions encountered on the Eastern Front, but these vehicles were also used later on the Western Front. On land the vehicle was driven normally, but once it entered the water the gears were set in neutral, the propeller arm was lowered, a sprocket engaged the crankshaft end and this drove a chain which in turn drove the propeller. Steering was effected by turning the front wheels. A total of 14,267 Schwimmwagens were built and production ceased in mid-1944. The Schwimmwagens all had the bigger 1,131-cc engine and weighed 1,992 lbs. The length was 12 ft $7\frac{1}{4}$ in., width 4 ft $10\frac{1}{2}$ in. and height with hood erected was 5 ft $3\frac{1}{2}$ in. Top speed of both these Volkswagens was 50 m.p.h.

20 Radio Truck, 4 × 4, Crossley Q, 1940–42, U.K.

While the British Army were later than the Germans and Americans in getting all-wheel drive vehicles into service (see Plates 48 and 106), the Royal Air Force had the Crossley Q 4 × 4 in service in mid-1940 sooner than any type ordered for the Army. Prior to 1941 the RAF looked after the procurement of its own transport through the Air Ministry and did not depend on the War Office in any way. Thus the RAF had several types of vehicle not used by the Army, of which the Crossley Q was one example. The Crossley was supplied in cargo, fire-tender, flat-bed, or ballast body forms, and also with a box body (mobile office) as shown. The particular vehicle drawn was equipped as a mobile fighter control unit for use on desert air strips in 1941–42. The Crossley Q was 20 ft 3 in. long, $7\frac{1}{2}$ ft wide, and 11 ft high.

21 Lorry, 4 × 2, 30 cwt, Anti-tank Bedford (armoured), 1940, U.K.

On May 10th 1940, Germany invaded France and Flanders using the 'Blitzkreig' tactics of armoured warfare which resulted in France's capitulation in just over a month. The British Expeditionary Force which protected the Flanders flank was forced back to the sea at Dunkirk and at the end of May the BEF was snatched from the Dunkirk beachhead by the famous armada of 'little ships'. In the speed of the withdrawal almost all the BEF's guns, tanks, trucks and armoured cars were of necessity left behind and were either destroyed or captured by the Germans. Britain was now left almost disarmed and was faced with a seemingly imminent invasion by German forces.

There were less than 100 tanks left in the country, most of them obsolete training vehicles. As a stop-gap while the factories built more tanks and armoured cars all sorts of road vehicles were acquired and given rudimentary armour protection ready to face the expected German tanks.

Some vehicles were produced as light armoured cars by fitting new partly enclosed bodies to staff car chassis.

A much cruder type, however, was the Armadillo, a generic name for a whole group of assorted types which were protected largely by wood since steel and armour plate were in exceptionally short supply. The Armadillo was designed by the London, Midland and Scottish Railway (whose plant, like so many other commercial concerns was given over to war work). Basically the Armadillo was a standard truck or lorry with a protected fighting compartment added. The Armadillo Mk I was the name given to an assortment of requisitioned commercial trucks of various makes and a total of 312 were converted in the summer of 1940. Many of these were used by the RAF for airfield defence. The next batch of vehicles to be similarly converted were about 300 Bedford 30-cwt and 3-ton army lorries. The protected box was made of two layers of stout wood with a 6 in. gap between the layers which was packed with pebbles. This gave a certain amount of protection from machine gun fire. Loopholes were provided for offensive fire by the crew, and light steel plates were fitted round the cab and engine. Some of the 3-ton vehicles were armed with a light gun and were called the Armadillo Mk III.

The third model produced was the type illustrated, the Bedford 30-cwt 'Lorry Armoured, Anti-tank'. This was similar to the Armadillo II but had steel plates instead of wood. The cab and bonnet were also more extensively armoured and further protection was given to the wheels and fuel tank. The armament was a Boys anti-tank rifle and a Bren gun (the former being shown). In the drawing the cut-down remains of the original cab and windscreen can be seen. These particular vehicles went to the divisions in south east England where the invasion could be expected, but fortunately the invasion never came and these crude improvisations were not put to the test.

Another type of extemporised armoured lorry at this period was the Bison which consisted of an old requisitioned heavy truck chassis with a concrete superstructure.

22 Truck, 4 × 2, 4 ton, Fordson Thames, 1940–44, U.K.

This vehicle was an ordinary commercial type which saw widespread military service. It was a conventional forward control vehicle with an all-steel tipping body. It was most extensively used by the Royal Air Force for airfield construction work and similar tasks. In addition to the end-tipper version shown there was a long wheelbase cargo truck and a prime mover for semi-trailers. One of General Montgomery's map caravans in 1944–45 was hauled by the prime-mover version, the semi-trailer being of the pantechnicon type. This particular vehicle is still preserved by the Ford Motor Co. in view of its association with Britain's most famous army commander of World War II. Yet another version of the Fordson Thames used by the RAF was the Tructor, a vehicle with a wooden dropside body and shortened chassis. It had towing gear and could be used for towing aircraft as well as for carrying air stores.

23 Bus, AEC Regent, 1940, U.K.

At the outbreak of war in September 1939 the British Army found itself very short of all kinds of motor transport. After the BEF's withdrawal from France the shortage became even more acute. Until production of new military vehicles built up the shortage was alleviated by the acquisition of large numbers of commercial vehicles. In 1940 buses were a favourite target since these could be used as excellent troop or personnel transporters of a kind. The divisions drawn up along the South Coast of England to defend the coast against the expected German invasion in the summer of 1940 were issued with large numbers of buses so that troops could be rushed quickly to any landing zone. The typical vehicle illustrated is a former Green Line coach which in this case is in use as an ambulance. Other buses were used as offices, command vehicles, and as mobile classrooms for training courses. The Royal Navy were big users of requisitioned buses for classrooms or training displays. For instance they had a mobile exhibition covering anti-aircraft defence of ships, and this visited dockyards all round Britain for the benefit of merchant ship crews.

24 Car, Light Utility, Standard 12 h.p., 1941–45, U.K.

Another of the light utility types in the same class as the Austin shown in Plate 17, the Standard was a slightly larger

vehicle being based on the Standard Flying Twelve, a very successful family car of the 1938–39 period. Only the bonnet and front wing pressings of the car were utilised in this vehicle, however, the rest of the bodywork being completely new. The cab was open with a canvas top and removable perspex side screens as in the larger GS trucks. The early production vehicles of the 1939–40 period had the radiator grille of the Flying Twelve car, but subsequent vehicles, as shown here, had a simplified wire mesh grille and slotted bonnet sides for cooling. The Standard Light Utility was one of the most successful of the various makes in its class and the type remained in use long after World War II, some being in Territorial Army service well into the 1950s. This vehicle had a four-cylinder 44 b.h.p. engine and was 13 ft 10 in. long. It was used by the RAF and Royal Navy as well as the army.

25 Truck, 8 cwt, FFW, 4 × 2, Humber, 1940, U.K.

The next class of vehicle above the light utility in British service use in the 1939–40 period was rated at 8 cwt. In appearance the vehicles concerned fell midway between the 15-cwt GS truck and the light utility. Since the 15-cwt chassis and the utilities between them could easily be used for the roles undertaken by 8-cwt trucks, this latter class of vehicle was dropped altogether in late 1941 in the interests of rationalisation. The major types on the 8-cwt chassis were both externally very similar. These were the GS (General Service) and FFW (Fitted For Wireless) types. They had a detachable well-type body with canvas tilt and folding legs by means of which the body could be stood on the ground. It could thus be used as a portable office, either as an office for (say) battalion HQ in the case of the GS version or as a wireless station. Vehicles in the 8-cwt class were made by Ford, Morris, and Humber. The early production Humber vehicles utilised the chassis of the civilian Humber Snipe limousine, 1939 production model. The bonnet and radiator grille were derived from the same vehicle. In the body at the rear was the standard No. 11 wireless set then in use, a table, and battery stowage for the radio. The batteries were re-charged from a generator driven off the main transmission. The GS vehicle had the same body but lacked the wireless fittings. A light ambulance body could also be fitted to this chassis. The Humber FFW had a six-cylinder 85 b.h.p. engine and was $14\frac{1}{2}$ ft long.

26 Motor-cycle Combination, BMW R75, 1940–45, Germany

In its basic form the BMW R75 motor-cycle combination was shown (as Plate 149) in the previous book in this series. It remained a major service type with the German Army for the whole of World War II but its importance diminished as time went on for its function as a reconnaissance vehicle was largely taken over by the VW Kubelwagen (Plate 18) and other light and medium car types. The illustration here shows a BMW R75 combination in use with a reconnaissance battalion of the Afrika Korps in the Western Desert in 1942 where a mixture of Kubelwagens and motor-cycles in the same unit was typical. Visible here are the valises on the sidecar which carried ammunition and

the crews' personal equipment, and the MG 34 machine gun on its bar mount on the sidecar. In desert operations it was practice to keep the breech of the gun covered to prevent sand getting in, and the gunner can be seen holding the canvas cover in place. In German terminology this heavy motor cycle and sidecar was known as a Schwerer Kraftrad mit Seitenwagen.

27 Sfl (Sd Kfz 7/1) with 2 cm Flakvierling, 1941–45, Germany

Development of the various classes of half-track prime mover produced in large numbers has been covered in the previous volume. Here we show some wartime developments—though the basic models of the 1930s continued in service and in production throughout World War II.

A major variant based on the Sd Kfz 7 8-ton half-track chassis was a self-propelled flak vehicle to give air defence to units in the field. This type of vehicle, designated Sd Kfz 7/1 appeared in 1941 and was essentially a Sd Kfz 7 gun tractor with the seats removed and replaced by a mount for the Flakvierling 38 quadruple 2-cm AA gun. This powerful weapon was a light hand controlled mount with a rate of fire from its four barrels combined of 800 rounds per minute. The side rails round the rear platform were covered by light wire mesh and opened sideways when the vehicle was cleared for action. For appearance of the standard Sd Kfz 7 tractor see Plate 132 in the previous volume in this series. The Sfl (Sd Kfz 7/1) —also known as the Mittlerer Zugkraftwagen 8t mit 2-cm Flakvierling 38— had a 10 man crew and weighed $11\frac{1}{2}$ tons.

Late production vehicles of this type (1943–44) had an armoured cab as shown in Plate 29.

28 Leichte Zugkraftwagen Sd Kfz 11 (Hanomag) converted to Ambulance, 1940–42, Germany

The basic 3-ton German half-track developed in the 1930s is also shown in the previous volume (Plate 127). This lighter type of half-track was not used as the basis of an AA vehicle, being mostly utilised as a gun tractor, munitions carrier, or decontamination vehicle. A few vehicles were, however, converted for a special role—the rescue of airmen whose aircraft were damaged in raids upon Britain and which came down in the sea en route to their base. The half-track configuration was chosen due to its suitability for operation on the beaches and dunes of Holland and France. These vehicles patrolled the coast with a rescue crew, medical stores, and dinghies aboard ready to aid any airmen spotted in the sea near the coast. In the distance is seen a Fieseler Storch spotter plane also used in the rescue work. These half-tracks were operated by the Coast Guard. The chassis was standard, with only the caravan-type body added.

29 Sfl (Sd Kfz 7/2) with 3·7 cm Flak 36, 1942–44, Germany

The second main type of mobile AA vehicle on the half-track tractor was originally (1941) based on the 5-ton (Sd Kfz 6) chassis which was the lightest type that could take the 2-ton weight of the 3·7-cm Flak 36 gun mount. In 1942, however, production of the 5-ton tractor was dropped and the Flak 36 gun was

henceforth fitted to the larger 8-ton chassis, the new type being designated Sd Kfz 7/2 (Mittlerer Zugkraftwagen 8t mit 3·7-cm Flak 36). Early vehicles had no armour protection and had the same appearance, with open sides and cab, as shown in Plate 27. The later vehicles had an armoured cab, an armoured shield for the radiator, and wooden dropsides replacing the tubular metal side rails of the earlier vehicle. The armoured cab was open at the back and extended rearwards far enough to cover the bench seat on which four members of the 7-man crew rode. Most vehicles had a shield for the Flak 36 gun, though there is not one on the example drawn. The addition of armour to these vehicles in the latter part of the war reflects the increasing dominance in the air of the Allied air forces on all fronts as the war progressed.

30 Ambulance, 1½ ton, 4 × 2, Chevrolet, 1940–42, U.S.A./U.K.

This widely used model was based on the commercial Chevrolet panel van and retained the 'Civilian' hood and grille but had heavy duty tyres and other military fittings. It could carry four stretcher or 10 seated patients. It equipped all arms of the American forces and was sent abroad under the Lease-Lend scheme and many were used by the British and Free French. The particular vehicle drawn has the markings of the Polish Division which served under British command. The Chevrolet 4 × 2 had a six-cylinder in-line engine giving 83 b.h.p. and was 24 ft long and 6 ft 10 in. wide. It went out of production in 1942 but remained in use until the war's end.

31 **Lorry, Ambulance, Indian Army Type, Australia,** 1941, Australia/India/U.K.

The small Australian Army prior to World War II obtained most of its limited numbers of military vehicles from Canada using what were basically commercial chassis, mainly Ford, Dodge, and Chevrolet. These chassis were imported in 'knocked down' form and assembled in Australia. Locally made bodies were fitted to suit required roles. This practice continued though on a larger scale in World War II. The vehicle shown is of 1941 vintage with the Australian Pattern fabric ambulance body. Cab, bonnet, and chassis were from the standard 1940 model Chevrolet light truck. This type of vehicle was widely used on Far Eastern fronts, particularly in India to which many vehicles of this type were supplied. Ordinary dropside cargo trucks were also built on this chassis, all in the 30-cwt class.

32 **Lorry, 3 ton, 6 × 4, Ford, with Balloon Winch,** 1940–44, U.K.

Like Austin (Plate 8) Ford produced a 6 × 4 chassis in the 3-ton class and this was fitted with several types of body ranging from cargo type to house type similar to that fitted to the Austin (Plate 104). A more characteristic role for this Ford, however, was as a winch lorry for barrage balloon operation. Many hundreds of this type of vehicle were used by the Royal Air Force to provide the power for the balloon barrages that protected key areas of Britain in the 1939–45 period. A separate petrol engine was mounted on the rear body to drive the enclosed winch drum and a mesh cage protected the winch operator from any breakage of the balloon cable during winding in or out operation. This vehicle was known as model WOT1 by Ford. It incorporated the normal Fordson commercial type pressed steel cab (cf. Plate 22) but had a WD pattern bonnet and mesh radiator grille. The V-8 85 b.h.p. engine was the same as that fitted in the commercial Fordson Thames truck of the period. Another special purpose type on the same chassis used by the RAF was a crash tender which featured a foam compound tank and high pressure delivery hoses and associated pumps.

33 **Lorry, 30 cwt, GS, 4 × 2, Dennis,** 1940–42, U.K.

This vehicle was built from commercial Dennis components to the 30-cwt rating for general use on airfields by the Royal Air Force. The cab and bonnet were identical to other current Dennis models. A wooden WD type body was fitted, plus a heavy duty towing pintle at the back. In service this vehicle, known as the Dennis AM (Air Ministry), was used for any task from carrying dustbins to towing bomb trailers. It had a four-cylinder, 75-b.h.p. engine and was 19 ft 10 in. long. This vehicle was not used in quantity by any other service.

34 **Light Artillery Tractor, 6 × 6, Dennis Octolat,** 1943–44, U.K.

The Octolat existed only in experimental prototype form and was designed to meet a requirement for a simple easy-to-produce and maintain gun tractor in place of the relatively complicated Quad tractors then in use for the field artillery. The design was novel, in particular in dispensing with conventional springs.

Any rough riding was absorbed instead by the giant tyres. The original plan allowed for eight wheels (hence the name Octolat) but these were reduced to six in order to keep the vehicle's weight and overall length to a minimum. The Octolat featured a simple platform body with a truck type cab on the prototype. This was replaced by a lightly armoured body with central control position and an overall canvas tilt. The body featured ammunition lockers. Power came from a 9·8-litre Leyland engine and the vehicle was about 20 ft long. Overall height was 7½ ft. The earlier vehicles had Twin-Bedford engines. No production order for this interesting vehicle was placed. The name Octolat was an abbreviation for eight (wheel) light artillery tractor.

35 Car, Heavy Utility, 4 × 4, Humber
36 Car, Heavy Utility, 4 × 2, Ford, 1941–44, U.K.

These were the principal British types of vehicle used as staff and command cars at every important level of command. While of generally similar size and shape, the Humber had four-wheel-drive unlike the Ford. The bodies were all steel and were six-seaters with four individual seats and two tip-up 'occasional' seats at the back. There was an opening two-piece tailgate and a folding map table behind the front seats. The two rear seats could be folded down to leave the body clear for load carrying when required. In the Western Desert both these types were sometimes modified to suit the climate by cutting off the roof and replacing it with a canvas folding tilt. The Humber had a six-cylinder,

4-litre engine of 85 b.h.p., the same power rating as the Ford which had a V-8 engine. The Humber was 14 ft 1 in. long while the Ford was 4 in. longer still. The Ford (designated WOT2 by the company) had a sliding sun-roof. This modification was made to some Humbers, also, especially to those used by high-ranking officers.

37 Truck, 15 cwt, GS, 4 × 2, Bedford
38 Truck, 15 cwt, Bedford, fitted experimentally with 20-mm Polsten Cannon
39 Lorry, 15 cwt, 4 × 2, Bedford (Mobile Tea Car), 1939–45, U.K.

The origin of the Bedford 15-cwt truck, one of the best known of all military vehicles, dates back to 1935 when the War Office held a trial for new types of lorry and invited Vauxhall Motors Ltd., makers of Bedford trucks, to enter the competition. The firm submitted a light van and their standard commercial 2-ton lorry. While the van gave an indifferent performance the 2-ton lorry proved to be the most efficient in its class, even against special military designs. Vauxhall accordingly fitted larger tyres and a larger 'colonial' style radiator and sent the vehicle to the Army for trials. With revision to the chassis to improve ground clearance and, later, modification to the cooling system the vehicle took part in the 1936 trials. By 1937 a purpose-built Bedford WD (War Department) prototype had been completed, still based on the 2-ton commercial chassis. This was rated at 15 cwt and was known as Model WD1 to Bedford. A distinctive feature was the simple squared-off bonnet which was fitted in place of the usual Bedford bonnet of the time in order to clear the extra-large air filter which the Army had specified. The bonnet was regarded as a temporary expedient for the trials but it was, in fact, retained for subsequent vehicles due to its simplicity and ease of production. In 1938 a more powerful engine was developed and fitted and contingency plans were made for production in the event of war. A provisional plan allowed for 2,000 15 cwts to be built within 6–7 months of an order being placed. In August 1939 the first 50 Bedford 15 cwts were ordered, all to be 'portées' for carrying 2-pdr. anti-tank guns. One of these vehicles is shown in Plate 147 in the previous volume. These vehicles had GS bodies but were fitted with ramps, chocks, and ammunition lockers. In September 1939 when war was declared the planned order for 2,000 vehicles was placed. Of these 480 were equipped as 'portées' and the others were built as GS trucks. Within a few weeks, however, new contracts were placed for 11,000 15-cwt trucks. Subsequently this number was considerably increased and Bedford 15 cwts made up to a large proportion of the 250,000 vehicles built by Bedford during the Second World War.

This 15-cwt chassis was known as the Bedford MW to its makers. The basic GS truck was mainly intended as a transport vehicle for the infantry platoon but it was, in fact, widely used by all arms. In its original form the Bedford 15 cwt had an open cab, folding 'aero' type windshields and canvas side screens. A folding hood gave limited cover in bad weather. From 1943, however, a more enclosed cab with side doors, a canvas top, and perspex side screens replaced the early open cab.

Overall length of the basic vehicle was 14 ft 4 in., and it was $7\frac{1}{2}$ ft high or 5 ft 3 in. without the folding cab top. The six-cylinder engine developed 72 b.h.p.

Several special purpose bodies were supplied on this chassis, including the mobile tea car shown (Plate 39) which was one of a group of vehicles purchased by public subscription for use by welfare services. The vehicle illustrated belonged to the Y.M.C.A. Another common type was the 200-gallon water tanker which is illustrated (Plate 148) in the previous book in this series.

One type which did not see widespread service was the Bedford 15 cwt fitted with the Polsten 20-mm gun to make a mobile AA mount. The Polsten was a rapid-firing machine cannon designed to supplement the Oelikon gun of 20-mm calibre. The gun barrel was put into production and Vauxhall were asked to design a suitable mount which could be used on the vehicle, removed and converted to a towed weapon, and broken down into basic components for mule transport. The lorry mount was also adaptable for ground firing. In this case the wheels— which were mounted on stub axles, were removed and jacks were fitted in their place. Design of this Polsten-gun mount started in June 1942 and the complete system was ready for test seven weeks later. Plans were made for 100,000 of these gun mounts, but due to lack of production facilities Vauxhall made only 100 for trials, training and demonstration. In the event this simple and effective weapon was not used in combat since the Allied air superiority of the last half of the war rendered mobile AA mounts of this nature quite unnecessary.

**40 Lorry, 3 ton, 4 × 2, Bedford
(Stores Van)**
41 Lorry, 3 ton, GS, 4 × 2, Bedford
**42 Lorry, 3 ton, 4 × 2, Bedford
(Bread Van),** 1940–45, U.K.

After the 8-cwt and 15-cwt lorries the
British Mechanisation Department planned new lorries in the 30-cwt and 3-ton
categories. The 30-cwt class was a continuation of the inter-war 'light lorry'
category but (as far as new models went)
in 4 × 2 rather than the old 6 × 4 configuration. The 3-tonners of the inter-
war period were also of 6 × 4 type
but the new building programme called
for 4 × 2 versions. Vauxhall, who
made Bedfords, had not had any service
contracts before the war and the 15-cwt
(Plate 37–79) was their first very successful effort. In May 1939 the firm was
asked to prepare to build 30-cwt and
3-tonners, again utilising existing commercial designs suitably adapted. Soon
after war broke out contracts were placed
for 5,000 30-cwt and 11,000 3-ton
vehicles. These were subsequently increased greatly and by 1945 over 250,000
Bedford trucks (of all sorts) had been
made. The 30-cwt trucks (see Plate 21)
were discontinued early on but the 3-
tonner became the major British service
type and Bedford were the main builders
with their famous Model OY. This
vehicle had the commercial type pressed
steel cab with the famous 'square nose'
bonnet (hood) that had been introduced
in the 15-cwt. The standard cargo truck
(Plate 41) had a wooden WD pattern
body which was later replaced by a steel
body (Plate 41).

There were numerous special bodies
and variants of the basic vehicle and two
of these are shown here. The stores van

126

(Plate 40) was mainly used at bases rather
than in the field and had a pantechnicon
body. The unusual bread van (Plate 22)
was used by field bakeries and could
carry 1,600 loaves fully loaded.

The Bedford OYD 3-tonner had a
six-cylinder, 72-b.h.p. engine and was
20 ft 5 in. long, 7 ft 1½ in. wide and 10 ft
2 in. high.

**43 Tractor, 6 ton, 4 × 2, Bedford,
with Torpedo Transporter Semi-
trailer**
**44 Tractor, 6 ton, 4 × 2, Bedford,
with 3-ton Aircraft Transporter
Semi-trailer**
**45 Tractor, 6 ton, 4 × 2, Bedford,
with 3-ton Cargo Semi-trailer**
46 3-ton Cargo Trailer, 1940–45,
U.K.

The Bedford OXC 6-ton prime mover
was a simple adaptation of the standard
30-cwt chassis which more usually
formed the basis of an ordinary load
carrier, and was also used for the 'lorry,
armoured, anti-tank' shown in Plate
21. Production of 30-cwt trucks was
reduced for military use after 1940 in
favour of the more useful and larger 3-ton
types. The 30-cwt chassis, however,
remained in production in its modified
form as a prime mover and was fitted
with the patent Scammell coupler for
semi-trailers which was automatic in
action and allowed the prime mover to
back up to the semi-trailer and couple up
automatically. It could similarly release
the semi-trailer to leave it for loading,
the weight at the front end of the trailer
being taken by roller-fitted retractable
arms fitted each side of the coupler. This
famous mechanical device will be familiar to everyone who has seen the mecha-

nical horses and trailers still used in parcels delivery work.

The British Army made relatively limited use of articulated load carriers in World War II. Such vehicles as were used were employed mainly at depots rather than in support of forward echelons. The major users of these Bedford 6-ton outfits were the Royal Navy and Royal Air Force for whom a number of special purpose trailers were built.

Plate 43 shows a Royal Navy vehicle with a torpedo carrier trailer which was used on naval air stations and for delivering torpedoes from ordnance depots. Above it is shown the Swordfish, most famous of the RN torpedo bombers. In Plate 45 is shown the same OXC prime mover with the standard WD pattern cargo trailer, which is more fully shown —with its Scammell coupling device— in Plate 46. This trailer was built by several firms to a standard design. Two other semi-trailers using the Scammell coupling device were a 1,750-gallon fuel tanker and a flatbed trailer. Both were supplied for the Bedford 6-ton prime mover.

Plate 44 shows what is probably the best known of all the wartime articulated vehicles, the 'Queen Mary' aircraft transporter semi-trailer. (The nickname owed its origin to the great 50-ft length of the semi-trailer.) Hundreds of these 'Queen Marys' were used by the Royal Air Force for the recovery of damaged aircraft or the delivery of new ones to airfields or depots. To the public the 'Queen Mary' was—and still is—a spectacular sight. The 'Queen Mary' trailer was of the low loading variety and was specially built by Taskers of Andover, the then well-known engi-

neering firm. It formed a cradle to hold an aircraft fuselage, and high outriggers could be fitted at the sides to support wings vertically. Small aircraft could be carried complete, as with the Spitfire illustrated, but very large aircraft required several trailers to carry the in sections. As an alternative to the Bedford, Crossley or Commer prime movers were used with the 'Queen Mary'. The Scammell coupling device was not used with the 'Queen Mary'. Instead a ball type flexible coupling designed by Tasker was used and the outfit was permanently coupled in normal circumstances.

The Bedford OXC model 6-ton prime mover remained in production until the end of the war. Some vehicles of this type were supplied in small numbers to commercial operators under wartime regulations and these were used either with the cargo semi-trailer or commercial type semi-trailers. Two non-service types of semi-trailer used in government 'works' service were a pantechnicon type enclosed load carrier with side and end doors and a bus or personnel carrier with side windows and wooden slatted seats for 50 passengers. A few of the latter were used by the Royal Navy, some converted to mobile classrooms for dockyard training use.

47 **Lorry, 3 ton, 4 × 2, 350 gallon Water Carrier, Bedford,** 1940–45, U.K.

A major type supporting forward echelons was the 'water bowser', the major standard Bedford OYC 3-ton chassis. The tank rested on a cradle attached to the chassis members and hand-worked pump on the side was used for filling and emptying when outside sources were not available. This water tanker was produced from 1941, but later it was given a heavier 500-gallon tank. A very similar looking vehicle was the petrol tanker version which had, however, a larger diameter tank of 800-gallon capacity. A metal framework was provided round the tank and in forward areas this was covered by a canvas tilt to disguise this important vehicle's true function from enemy aircraft and artillery.

48 **Lorry, 3 ton, 4 × 4, Fire Tender, Bedford**
49 **Lorry, 3 ton, 4 × 4, Mobile Laboratory, Bedford**
50 **Lorry, 3 ton, 4 × 4, Mobile Canteen, Bedford**
51 **Lorry 3 ton, 4 × 4, Command Vehicle, Bedford**
52 **Lorry 3 ton, 4 × 4, Mobile Dental Surgery, Bedford,** 1940–45, U.K.

Probably the most famous of all British World War II army lorries was the very familiar square-fronted Bedford QL (QL being Bedford's model designation). This vehicle was actually developed specially for military use, in contrast to the 15-cwt, 30-cwt, and 3-ton 4 × 2 models which were all basically adaptations of commercial designs. Apart from a few experimental types and the American FWD of 1918 vintage, the British Army had not previously used four-wheel-drive (4 × 4) vehicles. The advantages of this type, both for on- and off-road work were obvious, however. Vauxhall's interest in this type of vehicle went back to December 1938

when development of the 15-cwt type was proceeding. Vauxhall's engineers suggested the feasibility of producing a four-wheel-drive Bedford and asked War Office permission to proceed with a design. Interest was expressed but there was no urgent requirement. However, work on a Bedford 4 × 4 vehicle proceeded on a 'low priority' basis. The outbreak of war in September 1939 gave a major boost to the project. Vauxhall's were asked to give top priority to producing the 15-cwt, 30-cwt, and 3-ton types, already described, as these were urgently needed. Meanwhile they were to proceed at once to build some prototype 4 × 4 models. The detailed specification was approved by October 1939 and on February 1st, 1940, the first prototype Bedford 4 × 4 truck was ready for trials, an astonishingly fast development period even by wartime standards. The Bedford QL (as it was later called by Vauxhall) was an entirely new design, but it proved to be almost entirely free from 'teething troubles' unlike many new models.

Production of the Bedford QL started in February 1941 and continued to the end of the war, by which time 52,245, had been built, a number which far exceeded the total for any other individual model.

Many different types of special bodywork were produced for the Bedford QL and five examples are shown here.

The Fire Tender (Plate 48) was similar to the basic 3-ton load carrier version, with steel GS body. The canvas tilt, however, concealed a most comprehensive set of fire fighting gear including ladders, hose-racks, tools and an auxiliary motor-driven pump built in at the back. This vehicle normally towed a

Dennis mobile fire pump. Fire Tenders were used by the Army Fire Service both in Britain and overseas to protect military installations.

The other vehicles shown here have various van-type bodies for special roles. The Mobile Canteen (Plate 50) was actually operated and manned by the N.A.A.F.I. (Navy, Army and Air Force Institute) for work in North West Europe after the Allied landings of June 1944. It was fitted out in the usual way for mobile catering, with tea urns, confectionery racks, and hotplates for dispensing snacks to off-duty soldiers and airmen. The Mobile Laboratory and Dental Surgery were used by Field Hospitals, the latter outfit being fully self-contained with the caravan trailer serving as a laboratory.

The Command Vehicle (Plate 51) is representative of a range of very important types which all had similar wooden 'house' bodies but were equipped for different roles. These included office, cipher office, wireless and wireless terminal vehicles. There were several detail differences between types, including varied door and window positions. A frequently seen fitting was a penthouse (tented) extension to each side of the body which was rolled up and attached to the body when the vehicle was on the move. A small petrol-driven generator and extra battery stowage was provided in the chassis of all these house-bodied vehicles to provide power for the wireless and lighting equipment. Bedford QLs of this type were the longest-lived of all wartime British vehicles and a few remained in service as late as 1970. A peace-time role which was found for some of these vehicles was as mobile recruiting offices and mobile

exhibition vehicles for Army display work. The actual vehicle drawn was a squadron commander's vehicle in the Berkshire and Westminster Dragoons (a Territorial unit) in 1965.

There were other important versions of the Bedford QL, among them a troop carrier with side doors and seats in the body, a prime mover for a 3-ton cargo trailer as shown in Plate 46, a gun tractor for a Bofors 40-mm AA gun, and a petrol tanker. The basic Bedford QL GS lorry was 19 ft 8 in. long, $7\frac{1}{2}$ ft wide, and 9 ft 10 in. high.

53 Lorry, 3 ton, 4 × 4, Bedford, experimental (Bedford Giraffe)
54 Lorry, 3 ton, GS (Bedford half-track), 1940–45, U.K.

These were two experimental versions of the Bedford QL which did not see service but are nontheless good examples of the ideas that were tried out to improve the potential of motor transport under combat conditions.

The Bedford Giraffe was an attempt to make a motor vehicle capable of very deep wading in river crossings and amphibious landings. A system of water-proofing vehicles for shallow wading was evolved during the war years, but there was a suspicion that this might not prove adequate. As a stand-by for production if needed, Vauxhall altered a Bedford QL so that its engine cab and gearbox were on an elevated girder framework 7 ft above ground level. Chain drive from the gearbox to the transfer box overcame the transmission problem. This proved most successful and would undoubtedly have been of value in ship to shore transfer of cargo had the need for such a vehicle arisen. As it happened the extemporised method evolved for waterproofing vehicles was successful and there was no further requirement for specialised types.

The Bedford Half-track (popularly called the 'Bedford-Bren') was a vehicle similar in conception to the German Opel Maultier (Plate 58). Its principal object was to dispense with the rear tyres at a time when rubber was scarce after the Japanese occupation of most of the rubber-producing countries of the East. The Ministry of Supply therefore took a standard Bedford QL and replaced the rear wheels with the track units from a Bren Gun Carrier. The rear axle of the Bedford was geared to drive the sprocket wheels of the track assemblies. The result was a vehicle of exceptional tractive power which could well have been produced in its own right as a standard type. However, the British military authorities, unlike the Germans (and the Americans at that time) did not favour the half-track mode of traction. As it happened the shortage of rubber was not so severe as had at first been envisaged and no further production or development took place with the Bedford-Bren.

55 Field Artillery Tractor, Bedford Traclat, 1940–45, U.K.

Though the British Army had chosen to standardise on wheeled artillery tractors, the huge success of the German half-track prime movers (see previous volume) particularly in the Western Desert campaign led to second thoughts on the subject. The German semi-tracked vehicles gave a very high 'go anywhere' standard of mobility which was used to good advantage in the fast deployment of the notorious '88' anti-tank guns that proved deadly against British tanks in several of the major desert engagements of 1942. Several German half-tracks were captured in good order, and one was sent to Vauxhall's for complete overhaul and testing. As a result of this work Vauxhall were asked to design a close copy of the standard German Sd Kz 7 half-track embodying all the features of the German vehicle but utilising as far as possible standard Bedford parts. The resulting vehicle was designated the Bedford BT (BT = Bedford-Tractor) and code-named 'Traclat' for 'Tracked light artillery tractor'. The vehicle was to be 'universal' in fittings to enable it to haul 17 pdr., 25 pdr., and Bofors guns with suitable stowage for the various types of ammunition.

Like the German half-tracks—described in the previous volume—this vehicle had drive to the sprockets and steered in the usual manner on the front axle. However, there was also a steering system linked automatically to the tracks which operated when the steering wheel went beyond a certain minimum lock. To provide the necessary power at minimal expense, two ordinary Bedford truck engines were used in the BT mounted side by side and geared to a common drive shaft. In many ways the BT was superior to the German original designs, particularly in its stowage arrangements. All lockers were accessible from outside the vehicle and space was well used. Even the space under the seats in the rear compartment was used for 'ready use' ammunition stowage.

Six Bedford Tractors were built for trials in 1944 and these were tested by the Army under conditions ranging from tropical to arctic. The vehicles gave an excellent performance, could climb a 1 in 2 gradient, wade to 6 ft deep, and had a speed better than 25 m.p.h. Plans for mass production were put in hand, but the war ended before any further progress was made in this connection. All contracts were cancelled and this promising design was prematurely terminated. The Bedford BT was 21 ft long, 7½ ft wide, and nearly 9 ft high. Total weight was 6 tons 16¼ cwt.

56 Car, Heavy Utility, Ford, 1940–45, Canada/U.K.

Yet another vehicle based on a civilian type vehicle, this was essentially the same as the Ford Heavy Utility shown in Plate 72 except that it was based on the 1941 production model rather than the 1942 model. Its typical estate car body differed slightly in styling from the 1942 version and it was less lavishly equipped for military work. Some vehicles of this type had roof hatches cut in and fuel and water racks attached on the outside. The V-8 engine was rated at 95 h.p. and the wheelbase and other details were the same as those of the 1942 model. This 1941 vehicle, at 4,230 lbs was nearly 200 lbs heavier than its successor, however. These cars were used by the Canadian and British Armies, most of those supplied to the latter being employed in the Western Desert and Italy. The particular vehicle shown was used in the Western Desert and portrays a favourite local modification, the removal of the complete roof. It also displays the red/white/blue air recognition sign used in 1942 in the desert, and the camel marking of the HQ Middle East.

57 Mittlerer Gelandegangiger Lastkraftwagen (Opel Blitz, A Type)
58 Gleisketten-Lkw, 2T, Maultier (Opel Blitz)
59 Mittlerer Personenkraftwagen (Opel Blitz) Wermachtbus, 1940–45, Germany

In the late 1920s the German Waffenamt (Ordnance Department) had drawn up a requirement for a general military load carrier in the 3-ton class with the 6 × 4 chassis configuration. This type of vehicle was very similar to the sort of truck being produced in Britain at that time. An advantage of the 6 × 4 layout was its relative simplicity, the drive being confined to the rear bogie, and the long high chassis which facilitated the fitting of specialist bodywork. Several manufacturers built trucks to this specification, including Krupp, Daimler-Benz, Magirus, and Henschel. The general appearance of the type is shown in Plate 122 of the previous volume which portrays the Henschel model. Daimler-Benz also produced some all-wheel drive vehicles of their own, some of which entered military service, and the Waffenamt also produced in 1936 its own design, the Einheitsdiesel, a 6 × 6 (all wheel drive) truck of sophisticated design which was intended as an eventual replacement for the 6 × 4 types. As its name implies this vehicle was diesel-engined, partly taking into account Germany's petroleum shortage—it all had to be imported—which might well become acute in the event of a blockade. (This petrol shortage became a grave reality, of course, later in the war.)

Together with the numerous designs being produced in other load categories, the German military transport inventory had become enormously costly and extremely complicated in terms of spare parts and maintenance by the late 1930s. There were over 100 truck types alone. In addition the new standard types like 'Einheitsdiesel' were very expensive to produce. To rationalise the motor transport situation, General von Schell who was Director of Mechanisation made major revisions in the military vehicle procurement programme. The aim was to cut down on the numbers of models used, to eliminate over-elaborate and costly designs, and as far as possible adopt designs which had both military and commercial applications. In the case of trucks the 100 or so different designs of earlier days were reduced to 30 basic models.

In the 3-ton (or medium) category the major and most successful design was the Opel Blitz. This was a 1938 design from Opel (the German subsidiary then, as now, of General Motors) and was quite conventional in layout. The Opel Model S3.6-36, to give its maker's designation, was a 4 × 2 vehicle with pressed steel cab and bonnet, a 3,626-cc six-cylinder engine developing 75 b.h.p., and a 5 speed gearbox. Suspension was by conventional leaf springs. Under the Schell Programme all the 4 × 2 vehicles were designated Type S (S = Standard). It was then planned to produce four-wheel drive versions of all standard types, predominantly for military use and these were designated Type A (A = Allradantrieb = all wheel drive). It was 1940 before the Type A variants went into production. In the case of the Blitz the wheelbase was shortened by 6 in. in the A variant and there was a two speed transfer gearbox

and front drive shaft added giving a choice of ten forward speeds. Externally, however, the two models appeared almost identical. Needless to say the Opel Blitz Type A had a reasonable cross-country performance and was designated 'mittlerer (gelandegangiger) Lastkraftwagen' (medium cross-country truck). The Opel Blitz was built in vast numbers. A total of 40,000 vehicles was scheduled for 1945 production alone. There were also, of course, many special purpose variants, over 100 different types being recorded. Most important of these featured a house-type body (Einheitskofferansbau) which could be fitted as a workshop, laundry, laboratory, command caravan, radio van, cipher office, ambulance, or for dozens of other purposes. The box-like house body was made of wood and compressed card, partly for ease of production and to save metal. Later in the Blitz's production life it was similarly fitted with the famous 'ersatz' cab, a wood and pressed card structure known as the 'einheitsfahrerhaus', again as a major economy measure when steel became short.

The standard Opel Blitz is shown in Plate 57, while Plate 58 shows another common vehicle the so-called 'Wermacht-Bus' which was a long (15 ft 3 in.) wheelbase version of the Blitz with an enclosed omnibus type body. Fitted with seats in the normal way it could carry 26 soldiers. The seats were removable and the vehicle could be fitted instead with stretcher racks to accommodate 23 men in the ambulance role (as illustrated). As yet another alternative it could be fitted as a command vehicle or map caravan for senior officers.

The third vehicle shown here (Plate 58), the Maultier (Mule) was developed by the Waffen-SS to overcome the severe mud and snow conditions of the Russian front which defeated even four-wheel drive. In what proved a successful experiment the complete track assemblies from obsolete Pzkpfw I light tanks were added to the rear chassis frames. The drive shaft was reduced in length and the axle was moved forward to line up with the sprocket wheels. The existing brake drums were retained for steering at the rear. It will be seen that the resulting vehicle was not unlike the British Bedford-Bren (Plate 54). The greatly improved performance led to the Maultier being adopted as a standard type. By mid 1943 there were 5,400 Maultiers in service though production ceased at this time in favour of purpose-built tractors for the Eastern front. Conversions to Maultiers were carried out on Fords, Daimlers and other types as well as on Opels.

The Opel Blitz remained a major type for many years. In 1943 Daimler-Benz commenced building Blitz's under licence in favour of the comparable Daimler design, and the Opel became the major German military truck of World War II. The Blitz continued in production well past the end of the war and in its S-Type form became the mainstay of post-war German commercial transport.

60 **Schwerer   Gelandegangiger Lastkraftwagen   (Büssing-NAG),** 1940–45, Germany

The Schell Programme of standardised trucks called for vehicles in the 1·5-ton, 3-ton, 4·5-ton, and 6·5-ton classes. Of these the 3-ton class was numerically

the most important and was covered by the Opel Blitz and other makes as described above. An exactly similar production arrangement was made for the heavy (schwerer) trucks in the 4·5 and 6·5-ton categories. Daimler-Benz, Büssing-NAG, Saurer, MAN, and Henschel produced designs to meet the specification in either one or both of the categories. The Büssing-NAG is representative of the whole series, being produced as either an S Type (4 × 2) or an A Type (4 × 4). It had a six-cylinder 105 b.h.p. diesel engine and was 26 ft 10 in. long. The vehicle shown was the model 4500A which was in production from 1941 on. As the model designation indicates this was a 4·5-ton vehicle, but Büssing-NAG also produced an externally similar vehicle in the 6·5-ton class.

61 **Schwerer Lastkraftwagen (o) (Tatra 6500/111),** 1940–45, Czechoslovakia/Germany

Despite the rationalisation brought about by the Schell Programme, the Wehrmacht still obtained numerous vehicles which fell outside the scope of this programme. For the most part these were types which emanated from countries like France and Czechoslovakia whose industries were turned to German use after their respective countries had been over-run. Czechoslovakia had a very advanced motor industry and was turning out some of the best cars, trucks, and tanks in the world when the country fell into German hands in 1939. For Germany the acquisition of a quantity of good quality military equipment and well equipped factories proved important. The standard Czech tank became an important standard German type (and in 1940 helped make up the numbers of tanks available for the campaigns of that year). Similarly a vast number of trucks served the Wehrmacht and remained in production for supply to Germany. The Tatra 6500 and 8000 models were externally similar, rated at 6·5 tons and 8 tons respectively. They were used as heavy cargo carriers by the German Army. They were about 28 ft long, had a V-12 diesel air-cooled engine, and were of the 6 × 4 type. The late production vehicle shown has the Einheitsfahrerhaus 'ersatz' cab which was introduced early in 1944. This was a wood and compressed card structure which replaced the earlier pressed steel cab, the object being to save steel which by this time was in very short supply. This same pattern cab—recognisable by its square box-like shape—was also fitted to most of the Schell Programme vehicles, including the Opel Blitz.

The (o) in the German designation of this vehicle stood for 'handelsüblich' which indicated a commercial type, i.e. a design outside the Schell Programme.

The Tatra 111 remained in production in Czechoslovakia for many years postwar and some are still to be seen in commercial service.

62 Lorry, GS, 15 cwt, 4 × 2, Dodge, 1940–45, Canada/U.K.

This Canadian-built Dodge 15-cwt was used by the Canadian Army, but it was supplied in larger numbers to the British Army and the Free French (one of whose vehicles features in the drawing), as well as other Allied armies. This type was particularly widely used in the

Western Desert by the British. The cab and bonnet were basically commercial pressings but the cab roof was made removable for shipping and/or operating. The body was all steel. There was also a water tanker version of this vehicle with a body similar to that shown in Plate 64. These vehicles were used for the same roles as the British-made equivalent types. The Dodge 15-cwt was 16 ft 9 in. long, 7 ft 1 in. wide, and had a six-cylinder 95 b.h.p. engine. There were also 30-cwt and 3-ton class Dodge trucks of similar type and with the same style of cab and bonnet.

63 **Truck, GS, 30 cwt, 4 × 4, Chevrolet C30**
64 **Truck, 15 cwt, 4 × 2, Water Tanker, Chevrolet C15**
65 **Truck, 8 cwt, 4 × 2, Wireless, Ford F8**
66 **Truck, 15 cwt, 4 × 4, Chevrolet C15A**
67 **Truck, Heavy Utility, 4 × 4, Chevrolet C8A**
68 **Truck, 3 ton, 4 × 4, Ambulance, Chevrolet C60L**
70 **Car, Heavy Utility, 4 × 2, Ford,** 1940–45, Canada/U.K.

Trucks made in Canada played a vital role in the British and Commonwealth war effort. Canada had a growing automotive industry in the immediate pre-war era, mostly by Canadian-based subsidiaries of major American firms. In pre-war years the very small standing Canadian Army used adapted commercial types of truck. Modifications included such features as heavy duty tyres and other military fittings. These were known as 'Modified Conventional' vehicles and the various Ford Utilities (Plates 56 and 72) and the Dodge trucks (Plate 62) were typical of vehicles in this category.

Canadian truck production really got into its stride after June 1940 when the British Army lost the greater part of its motor transport and tanks in France at the time of the Dunkirk evacuation. With British industry already fully stretched and Britain under the threat of invasion and bombing, the British Government looked to Canada as a source of fresh supplies. Both tanks and motor vehicles were ordered in large numbers and this was the beginning of Canada's large scale involvement in military truck production.

The need for increased numbers of military vehicles in the event of hostilities had been to some extent foreseen in the mid-thirties and export models of several types of truck were already being supplied to such Commonwealth or British-protected countries as Australia, India, South Africa, and Egypt. Subsequently the two largest vehicle builders, Ford and General Motors, decided to pool their designs in the event of future emergency production. As a result of this a series of designs known as Canadian Military Pattern types were worked out by Ford and General Motors (Chevrolet) in conjunction with the Canadian War Department's Army Engineering Design Branch. The range corresponded exactly with the classes then (1938–40) being evolved and produced in Britain, namely 8-cwt, 15-cwt, 30-cwt, 3-ton trucks and field artillery tractors. Utilities, ambulances, and other special bodied types were to be produced on these various chassis also. The truck bodies were of the general service

(GS) type corresponding in style to their British equivalents.

Externally the CMP vehicles looked all alike, differing only in small details like the grille or the makers' badges. Internally they differed in having either a Ford V-8 engine and transmission, or a Chevrolet straight six engine and transmission, according to manufacturer.

The first CMP production vehicles were ready by the beginning of 1940 and first equipped the expanding Canadian Army. By mid 1940 supplies were being sent to British and Commonwealth troops in the Middle East and some were arriving in Britain. By 1941 production had reached a mammoth scale with nearly 190,000 vehicles completed. A year later this had reached nearly 200,000. Total truck production by 1945 was over 815,000 and CMP trucks formed numerically an important proportion of British and Allied vehicle strength.

During the 1940–45 production period there were a few major changes in design, the main one being a change of cab and bonnet which was quite distinctive. The early cab was known as the CMP No. 11 and was of fairly conventional appearance, well shown in Plate 64. It was side opening and the headlamps were mounted on the wings. A slightly modified type was the CMP No. 12, shown in Plate 63, which differed in having a bonnet that opened from the top in so-called 'alligator' style. This original type of cab was criticised by its users for being cramped, and restricted. This led to the introduction in 1942 of a new pattern cab, CMP No. 13, which was wider and incorporated the headlamps in a widened bonnet. There was a wider deeper windscreen which sloped forward very distinctively and is well shown in Plate 66. Various modified versions of these cabs also existed (e.g. open-topped types) but these were relatively rare.

The vehicles shown here are just a few typical CMP models illustrating major types.

Plate 63 shows the 30-cwt, 4 × 4 model, in this case with CMP No. 12 cab. The same vehicle was built with the No. 11 and No. 13 cabs, and was produced by both Chevrolet (C30) and Ford (F30). It was also made with an AA tractor body, a mobile office, and a Portee for 2-pdr. anti-tank gun. It was 16½ ft long and the Chevrolet six-cylinder engine was rated at 85 b.h.p.

Plate 64 shows a water tanker on the 15-cwt chassis and with the same 200-gallon tank as on British 15-cwt WD type water tankers. In Plate 66 is shown an 8-cwt wireless truck exactly similar to British types (see Plate 25). The body was removable and could be supported on folding jacks. A petrol driven generator for charging the radio batteries could be carried in the space between the body and the cab.

There was also a personnel carrier version of this vehicle with similar body. The 15-cwt cargo truck in its 4 × 4 form is shown in Plate 66. The example drawn has the CMP No. 13 cab and steel body. Early models had the CMP No. 11 or 12 cab and a wood body. A variant had an office body of the canvas covered kind which was externally similar to the GS truck. Plate 68 shows the 3-ton, 4 × 4 ambulance model which had a house-type body for four stretchers or 10 sitting cases. This vehicle was 19 ft long and 7½ ft wide. Cargo, GS truck, tipper, office, dental surgery, breakdown, and

petrol tank versions of this model were produced. Finally Plates 67 and 68 show versions of the heavy utility trucks built on CMP chassis. The major type was the 8-cwt, C8A 4 × 4 model which entered production in 1942. It was a very popular, well-equipped type used by all arms in the command and liaison roles. The body was all steel. Ambulance, staff car, wireless, and machinery and light repair versions were also built using the same basic body. The 4 × 2 model (Plate 70) was used mainly in the personnel carrying role and was an early production type, the body being built in Britain on the basic 8-cwt chassis.

The field artillery tractor built in the CMP range is covered earlier in Plate 2. As can be seen from just the few examples included here, the flexibility of the CMP range was remarkably complete with maximum interchangeability of parts which took full advantage of the highly developed flow line production systems used by the Canadian truck manufacturers.

69 Lorry, 15 cwt, 4 × 2, Water Contamination, Morris CS8, 1940–45, U.K.

A less well-known type of special purpose truck, this vehicle was based on the standard Morris-Commercial 15-cwt chassis (Plate 154 in previous volume). It resembled a water or fuel bowser but its true function was the more sinister one of water contamination—rendering all drinking water outlets unusable to the enemy. In 1940 when invasion threatened at any moment, numbers of these vehicles were held ready to descend on water points, water mains, rivers, streams, and other sources of water supply, there to release chemicals into the water to render it unfit for human consumption. Only small numbers of these vehicles were built and this type of truck was dropped at an early date due to the very limited use to which it could be put.

71   **Car, Light Sedan, Ford 21A**
72   **Car, Heavy Utility, 4 × 2, Ford,** 1942, U.S.A./Canada/U.K.

This is another example of a basically commercial type which was put into military service in large numbers with only small changes to suit it to army requirements. Ford of Canada produced this type mainly for British use, though many were also used by the Canadian Army. It was based on the 1942 Ford Fordor station wagon which was one of the Ford range of cars then sold in U.S.A. and Canada. For military service it was given right-hand drive (since it was principally for delivery to Britain), heavy duty tyres, shielded headlamps, simplified and strengthened fenders front and rear, roll-up blackout blinds, rifle racks inside, and other military standard fittings, including a first aid locker. It could carry up to six passengers plus the driver. In service this vehicle was mainly used by HQ staffs in all types of formation. Many were used by senior officers. A roof rack was a standard fitting though this was sometimes removed, as in the vehicle illustrated.

On the same chassis both Ford of Canada and Ford U.S.A. built their ordinary Fordor sedan for military use, mainly as a staff car. This vehicle had the same changes as the utility to suit it for

military use. The front end was identical but the staff car had the stock three-light saloon body. Canadian-built sedan had right-hand drive while U.S. built vehicles—used only by U.S. forces—retained the original left-hand drive and were standard in every way, with the 'stock' tyres and fenders. All these Ford Fordor-based vehicles had a wheelbase of 114 in., a 95-h.p. V-8 engine and were 16¼ ft long and 6 ft 1 in. wide (6 ft 7 in. in the heavy utility).

73   **Kleine Kettenkraftrad, Sd Kfz 2**
74   **Kleine Kettenkraftrad Sd Kfz 2/1 (Line-layer)**
75   **Kleine Kettenkraftrad Sd Kfz 2 (used as gun tractor),** 1940–44, Germany

The so-called Kleine Kettenkraftrad (small tractor) was unique in being virtually a half-track motor-cycle. It was designed by the Waffenamt (German Ordnance Department) in 1940 specifically to provide a light transport vehicle for parachute units. In practice it was built to the maximum dimensions and weight which allowed it to be carried inside a Junkers 52 three-motor transport aircraft, which was the standard troop carrier of the Luftwaffe. The front forks and fittings came from a motor-cycle while the track units were a small scale version of the tracks used on the normal half-track tractors. A 1·5-litre Opel 36-b.h.p. four-cylinder car engine was used as the power unit. Seats were provided for the driver and two passengers, and the bodywork (which also incorporated the rear seats) was in pressed steel. The vehicle was built by NSU, the well-known motor-cycle firm, and went into service in 1941. It was first used on active service in the airborne landings at Crete the same year. The vehicle was used principally as a supply and ammunition carrier or as a tractor for the lightweight anti-tank guns or howitzers (Plate 75) used by Luftwaffe parachute regiments. The Sd Kfz 2 remained in use with the parachute divisions until the end of the war even though these divisions were rarely used in the airborne role after 1941. Production ceased in 1944. A few of these vehicles also found their way into army hands and were used for instance in North Africa and on the Russian front.

Variants were the Sd Kfz 2/1 and the very similar Sd Kfz 2/2 (Plate 74), which were telephone cable layers with a cable reel carried in a cradle over the central engine compartment. The differences between these two were in the type of cable, light and heavy respectively.

The Sd Kfz 2 was 9 ft 10 in. long, 3 ft 2½ in. wide, and 3 ft 10¾ in. high. It weighed 1,560 kilograms and had a top speed of 80 km.p.h. There were six forward gears and two reverse.

76 Heavy Artillery Tractor, 6 × 4, Albion CX22, 1940–45, U.K.

The Albion artillery tractor was produced to meet the same requirements as the Scammell tractor shown in Plate 80. The Albion CX series was produced from 1940 onwards and as with the Scammell there was also a tank transporter variant. These Albions were never as popular as the Scammells, however, being rather heavier and less powerful. The Albion CX series first saw service, in fact, in its tank transporter

role where it proved to be somewhat unsatisfactory. The artillery tractor version replaced it in production and first entered service early in 1944. It never replaced the long serving Scammell, however, though this model of Albion remained in post war service for some years. A better known, and more successful vehicle was the Albion 10-ton cargo truck (model CX23N) which had the same engine and was of similar appearance to the gun tractor except that it had a forward control cab and a correspondingly longer body.

The Albion heavy artillery tractor was used mainly to tow the 7·2-in. gun or the 6-in. howitzer. It had a six-cylinder 100 b.h.p. diesel engine, was 25½ ft long, and weighed just over 10½ tons. It could carry a gun crew of 10 men, plus battery stores and 'ready-use' ammunition. There was a roof hatch in the cab for observation or AA defence with a machine gun.

77 Tank Transporter and Recovery, 30 ton, Tractor and Semi-Trailer, Scammell
78 Tractor Heavy Breakdown, 6 × 4, Scammell SV/2S
79 W.D. Pattern rubber overall tracks for Scammell Rear Bogie
80 Heavy Artillery Tractor, 6 × 4, Scammell, R.100
82 Tractor, Heavy Breakdown, 6 × 4, Scammell, SV/1T, 1940–45, U.K.

The Scammell series of vehicles were the longest serving of all in the British Army. The Scammell Pioneer, which first featured the famous Scammell articulating rear bogie, appeared in the late

1920s and the model R.100 heavy artillery tractor in its finalised form entered service in 1937. It has already been described and illustrated in the previous volume, but it is here shown (Plate 80) in its service form as it appeared in 'warpaint' in 1944. Towing a 7·2-in. gun, the vehicle illustrated belonged to one of the AGRAs (Army Group Royal Artillery) serving in Italy under 1st Army command. It has an 'A' battery sign on the cab roof. The body was similar to that shown in Plate 76 except that it had a hard metal-panelled top. A gantry ran the length of the body inside for handling ammunition and stores. These gun tractors served until 1945 and beyond and many remain in use today, 'demobilised' as showmen's or fairground tractors.

The Scammell chassis also formed the basis of the British Army's standard heavy breakdown tractor replacing an assortment of earlier types which lacked the power and lifting capacity for the new heavier vehicles which entered service after 1940. The early model SV/1T (Plate 82) had a folding rear jib which was fixed in one position and had an 8-ton winch behind the cab. This was quickly superseded by the model SV/2S (Plate 78) which became the major type. It had a jib with an arm which could be extended rearwards and fixed in any of three positions. A hand winch on the jib supports adjusted the arm to the required position. At maximum extension the jib would lift 2 tons, at its middle position it would lift 3 tons, and at the inner position up to 8 tons. In order to keep the front of the vehicle on the ground, heavy pig iron weights could be slotted in various combinations to a girder bracket on the radiator front.

On this vehicle there were two large stowage boxes which formed the bodywork each side of the jib. These acted as tool boxes and also carried extra ballast weights. There was also an outfit of rigid towing arms which could be used for hauling lighter types of vehicle. An 8-ton winch, driven via power take-off from the transmission, was located inside the chassis. The Scammell breakdown tractor was a most useful and versatile vehicle, used on every front and in all kinds of situations. Though used predominantly for recovering disabled wheeled vehicles, skilful handling by a team of three Scammells could also right an overturned tank. For heavier work some Scammells were provided with a wedge-shaped earth anchor (which attached at the rear of the chassis members) and rubber and chain overall tracks (Plate 79) which could be fitted over the rear wheels as shown in Plate 78/79. These turned the vehicle into what was virtually a half-track though they were not universally liked. Plate 78 shows the exceptional flexibility of the Scammell's suspension system, achieved by the heavy transversely sprung front axle and the independently sprung articulating rear bogie.

The Scammell heavy breakdown tractor had an exceptionally long service career, some remaining in use until the late 1960s. Very many ex-Army vehicles were sold commercially and remain a quite common sight as service station recovery vehicles. The Scammell Heavy Breakdown Tractor was 20¼ ft long and 9½ ft high. It weighed about 10 tons.

Last of the famous Scammell series was the Tank Transporter and Recovery Vehicle (Plate 77) which was produced as a complete outfit made up of the 6 × 4 tractor itself and a 30-ton semi-trailer with folding ramps. The trailer was pivoted on a turntable on the tractor. An 8-ton winch in the chassis led its whip back over a sheave on the semi-trailer end and could be used to haul (or assist) immobilised vehicles on to the trailer. There was a crew shelter just behind the tractor cab. The first Scammell recovery vehicles were in service in 1940 and the type was very widely used in all theatres. There was a similar combination with a 20-ton semi-trailer. Total weight of the 30-ton semi-trailer and tractor was just under 20 tons, and the overall length was 49 ft 8 in.

All the Scammell vehicles had a six-cylinder Gardner diesel engine of 8·3 litres rated at 100 b.h.p.

81 Field Artillery Tractor, 4 × 4, Morris C8, 1940–45, U.K.

This was the final production version of the Morris-Commercial C8 artillery tractor. Mechanically it was identical to the early model (Plate 1). In 1944 a greatly revised body was fitted, very much simpler than the original enclosed type. The top was open with a canvas cover, and there were two doors each side. The rear end of the body was squared off and was given ammunition racks of a 'universal' type, able to hold either 25-pdr. or 17-pdr. rounds. The vehicle could be used thus as a tractor for either the 25-pdr. gun-howitzer or the big 17-pdr. anti-tank gun, the idea being to standardise on one type of tractor for guns of comparable size. This type of tractor remained in service until the early 1950s.

83 Scammell Petrol Bowser for Bedford 6-ton Prime Mover, 1940–45, U.K.

Plates 45 and 46 show a typical combination based on the Bedford OXC prime mover. Another semi-trailer designed to be hauled by the same tractor unit was a fuel tank (or bowser). Various capacity tanks were supplied, mostly by Scammell whose patent articulated coupling (clearly shown in this drawing) was fitted to the Bedford tractor unit. This meant that one tractor could handle more than one semi-trailer, thus ensuring maximum utilisation of the tractor (i.e. empty trailers could be left for loading while full trailers were carted away).

The parked trailer was supported on the 'jockey' wheels visible in the drawing. These were automatically retracted once the tractor unit backed up and engaged the coupling. The tanker semi-trailer shown is the type supplied to the Royal Navy and was used for aviation fuelling on naval airfields. It had a hand-operated pump. The British Army used a different model tanker trailer which had a frame for a bogus tilt to disguise the vehicle's purpose.

84 Truck, 2½ ton, 6 × 4, Cargo, Studebaker
85 Truck, 2½ ton, 6 × 6, Cargo, GMC
86 Truck, 2½ ton, 6 × 4, Cargo, GMC
87 Truck, 2½ ton, 6 × 6, Cargo Dump, GMC
88 Truck, 2½ ton, 6 × 6, Gasoline Tank, Studebaker

89 Truck, $2\frac{1}{2}$ ton, 6 × 6, Cargo, GMC, 1940–45, U.S.A.

In the United States, after a few attempts to build prototype standardised vehicles by the Quartermaster Corps in the twenties and early thirties, the Comptroller General of the War Department finally decided that all such activities should cease as an economy measure. The Chiefs of Staff were also in favour of giving up efforts to evolve standardised truck designs because the only earlier attempt to produce such vehicles (the Liberty series of 1918—see previous volume) had ended in fiasco with long delays, wasted effort, big expenditure and little to show in terms of completed trucks.

However, the years 1930–34 saw some useful progress towards the idea of a standardisation policy, and the Quartermaster Corps managed to draw up on paper a 'standard' fleet of 18 types of vehicle which could be assembled using readily available components. The Ordnance Department opposed such plans saying that if an emergency arose there would not be time to put any standardised types into production. By the Spring of 1934, therefore, all this activity was abandoned and the Quartermaster Corps —responsible for all motor transport procurement—were told to buy ordinary commercial types suitable for military use.

Ironically enough, however, the German Schell Programme of 1938 (see Plates 57–60) was thought to have been originated after senior German officers read detailed reports of the Quartermaster Corps' original 'standardisation' proposals of 1930–34.

In the U.S. Army, the new policy of commercial purchasing led to the opposite extreme. By 1935, after only a year of commercial buying the vehicle inventory numbered 360 different types requiring the stocking of nearly one million different types of spare parts, a situation which was almost impossible to administer.

By 1939 this led to an arrangement whereby purchase of each type of vehicle would be restricted to two different competing commercial makes. Vehicles bought were to be ordinary standard commercial types with military modifications restricted only to towing eyes and radiator and headlamp guards. Procurement was limited to five basic vehicle capacities, $\frac{1}{2}$ ton, $1\frac{1}{2}$ ton, $2\frac{1}{2}$ ton, 4 ton, and $7\frac{1}{2}$ ton. By competitive bidding, also, they reduced the number of makes purchased in 1941 to just 16. Encouragement was given to these firms to utilise common accessories and mechanical parts.

By June 1940, following the new stipulations the Quartermaster Corps had tested and approved types in three of the new classes, namely Dodge 4 × 4 $1\frac{1}{2}$ ton, General Motors (GMC) 6 × 6 $2\frac{1}{2}$ ton, and Mack 6 × 6 6 ton. By this time Europe was at war with the possibility of American involvement in the not too distant future. America now began a vast re-armament programme and as an emergency measure the competitive bidding system for truck orders was dropped in favour of negotiated contracts. However, bureaucratic delays meant that this system didn't come into use fully until the middle of 1941. Truck production then soared to unprecedented quantities and overall the United States produced far more transport vehicles than either Germany or Britain.

In July 1940 the U.S. Army had 30,000 trucks and by January, 1941 it had 70,000. By December 1941 the total was over 250,000.

Of all the types of truck produced the dominant class was the 2½-tonner 6 × 6, of which over 800,000 had been built in America by the end of the war in 1945. The first 2½-tonners were of the COE type, ordered in late 1940 and entering production in January 1941—based on a commercial vehicle. This early type of 2½-tonner (which nonetheless remained in production throughout the war) is shown in Plate 13. The more widely known version had a normal control layout and examples of the models produced are given in Plates 84–89.

In addition to the COE type, Yellow Truck and Coach Co., the first builders received contracts for normal control 2½-tonners in September 1941. (This firm was partly owned by GMC and became wholly owned in 1943.) The initial mass production model (Plate 85) featured a commercial pressed steel cab (with AA gun ring in the roof), but the original commercial bonnet (which was carried by early production vehicles) was replaced by a much simpler pressed steel bonnet of squared-off and simplified shape. Due to the size of the ensuing contracts, the relatively small Yellow Truck Co. was unable to handle all the production, and Studebaker were called in to share the work at the end of 1941. The Studebaker 6 × 6 (Plate 88) utilised a slightly different pressed steel cab and had a different make of engine (Hercules). Due to its slightly non-standard nature the Studebaker was allocated to Lend-Lease and the majority were shipped overseas. Over 100,000 were sent to Russia alone. Other firms engaged in making 2½-tonners were Reo and International Harvester Co.

As production progressed the all steel cab was gradually replaced by a soft canvas-topped roof and side screens (Plate 87).

The 6 × 6 arrangement of these 2½-tonners was considered difficult to produce at first due to the use of all-wheel-drive which had not been built in such vast numbers before. However, this was soon resolved and with its excellent tractive capability the 6 × 6 2½-tonner proved to have an excellent off-the-road performance. Parallel to the 6 × 6 vehicles GMC and Studebaker both made 6 × 4 versions of the 2½-tonner with no front wheel drive. These were used for ordinary haulage work where the need to leave the road was unlikely. Externally they were identical to their 6 × 6 counterparts save for the lack of a live front axle. Plates 86 and 84 show examples.

The 2½-tonner was numerically the most important army truck of World War II and it was supplied under Lend-Lease to Canada, Britain, Free French and most other Allied nations. Variants included the normal steel-bodied cargo truck, a water tanker, gasoline tanker (Plate 88), dumper and the cargo-dump truck, a multi-role type with tipping cargo body (Plate 87). The 2½-tonner came with a 145-in. wheelbase in normal control form or 164-in. in COE form. A typical vehicle had a 104 b.h.p. six-cylinder GMC engine, 5 forward gears, and reverse. Overall length was 21 ft and width 7 ft 4 in. Vehicles were built with or without a front-mounted winch.

The 2½-tonner remains in production to this day with progressive modifications. Popular nicknames applied to it include 'Eager Beaver', 'Deuce and a half' and 'Jimmy'.

90   Truck, ½ ton, 4 × 4, Ambulance, Dodge, 1940–45, U.S.A.

In the ½-ton category of truck Dodge were the exclusive builders for the U.S. Army. Chrysler's Fargo Division (Dodge) were one of the first vehicle manufacturers to receive contracts under the re-armament scheme when they were given an order for 14,000 ½-ton 4 × 4 trucks in the summer of 1940. The basic chassis was similar to the existing Dodge commercial design except for the addition of the transfer gearbox and new front transmission to give four-wheel-drive. A very large number of body styles was produced, this vehicle being roughly equivalent in function and use to the British 15-cwt. Pick-up radio, command, command reconnaissance, panel van, weapons carrier, and ambulance were the main types built, appearing with or without a hard top cap according to type—the command, command reconnaissance, radio, and weapons carrier types were open cab models. The vehicle shown is the ambulance model and the panel van model was similar in shape but had a narrower body.

Production of ½-ton 4 × 4 trucks continued until 1942 when a new ¾-ton category was introduced. At this time ½-ton truck production ceased after 82,000 units had been built.

The Dodge ½-tonner had a six-cylinder engine rated at 85 b.h.p. and four forward speeds. In ambulance form it was 16 ft 3 in. long, and 6 ft 4 in. wide. This vehicle was also supplied to some other nations under Lend-Lease.

91   Truck, 6 ton, 4 × 4, Cargo, FWD, 1940–45, U.S.A.

Though used in small numbers by the U.S. Army, this very big powerful vehicle was supplied in even larger quantities to the British and Canadian Armies. The FWD was the latest model of a line of four-wheel-drive trucks dating back to 1914 and illustrated and described in the previous volume. It was basically a commercial model included among the initial U.S. Army orders for trucks in the 6-ton class placed in 1941. In U.S. Army service it was supplied in the cargo form illustrated, in slightly modified cargo form with sheerlegs as a pontoon bridge carrier, and with a low ballast body to pull low loader tank transporter trailers. The bridge carrier had demountable sheerlegs which were erected on the body sides to swing pontoons and girders over the tailgate of the vehicle.

When the initial U.S. Army contract expired in late 1942 no further FWD orders were placed for home use. However, the FWD type continued in production for Lend-Lease purposes, most vehicles going to Britain. Those supplied to Britain were sent either as cargo vehicles in the form illustrated or as cab/chassis units to which the British added standard WD pattern medium artillery tractor bodies as fitted to the Matador (Plate 3). A few ballast body tractors were also supplied to Britain.

The FWD proved tough and durable and as late as 1970 some were to be seen in commercial service as showman's tractors.

The FWD had a 126-b.h.p. Waukesha six-cylinder engine and a 12 ft wheelbase. In the cargo form shown it was 21½ ft long and 8 ft wide. The artillery tractor version was 8 in. longer. An unusual feature of the FWD was its permanent fixed four-wheel-drive without the usual option of two-wheel-drive for road running.

92 Truck, 2½ ton, 6 × 6, GMC, COE Type, 1940–45, U.S.A.

This vehicle was the late production version (1943–45) of the Yellow Truck and Coach Co's forward control ('cab over engine'—COE) model in the 2½-ton truck programme. The COE type went into production in early 1941 and originally had a commercial type hard top cab (Plate 13). To facilitate shipping and save metal this was dropped in early 1943 and most types of truck were given an open-sided doorless cab and a folding canvas cab cover with perspex and canvas sidescreens. Apart from its longer (15 ft or 17 ft) body and forward control layout the vehicle was mechanically the same as that shown in Plate 85. For a comparison with the earlier version of the COE type 2½-tonner see Plate 13. This vehicle had folding wooden seats along the body insides for use in the troop carrying role.

93 Truck, 4–5 ton, 4 × 4, Federal with 10-ton Refrigerated Trailer, 1940–45, U.S.A.

In the 4–5-ton class basic commercial types were once again ordered in the 1941 rearmament programme. These were conventional 4 × 4 prime movers used for long distance road haulage. The major builders were Federal and Auto-

car (whose vehicles looked very similar) and Kenworth and Marmon-Herrington.

The initial production models had enclosed pressed steel cabs but from 1943 the open-topped cab was adopted with a folding canvas cover and folding windscreen. An anti-aircraft machine gun mount was a common, but not universal fitting.

Three types of semi-trailer were produced, namely 2,000-gallon gasoline tanker, box van, and refrigerated van. The refrigerator van had its own built-in petrol-driven generator to operate the cooling plant.

These articulated outfits were built in large numbers for the big supply routes, like the 'Red Ball Highway', which were set up in France in 1944 to speed supplies from the channel ports to the fighting fronts. On these supply routes a continuous stream of convoys operated round the clock in one of the largest road transport operations ever known. In fact it was the smooth organisation of these major supply lines that was a prime factor in the final Allied victory over Germany.

The Federal tractor was 17 ft long and 8 ft wide. It had a Hercules 112-b.h.p. engine.

94 Bus, 2½ ton, 4 × 2, International K7, 1940–45, U.S.A.

Based on the type of bus already sold commercially, this was the most widely used of several makes. It was a 37-seater though some vehicles of this type had their seats stripped out and were used as ambulances. It featured the standard International Harvester chassis of the period which in shortened form formed the basis of a truck. An improved model, the KS7 had a two-speed rear axle. The vehicle was 32 ft long and had a six-cylinder, 87½-h.p. engine.

95 **M2 High-Speed Tractor, 7 ton, Cletrac,** 1940–45, U.S.A.

The Cletrac tractor was specially built as a tug for aircraft at U.S. Army, Air Force and Navy stations. It carried full road equipment—lights and mud-guards—to make it suitable for driving on public roads. It had a Hercules six-cylinder 137 b.h.p. engine of the type fitted in heavy trucks and featured a compressor for braking purposes. The bogies were of the sprung volute type and there was an all steel track. The cab was normally left open, as illustrated, but canvas weather screens and top were provided for inclement conditions. Weight was 7 tons and the overall length was 14 ft 2 in., width just under 6 ft. A few of these vehicles were supplied to the Royal Air Force.

96 **Truck, 1½ ton, 4 × 4, Bomb Service Vehicle**
97 **Bomb Handling Trolley,** 1940–45, U.S.A.

While 1½-ton trucks of commercial type had been purchased by the U.S. Army in the 1930s it was not until 1940 that the 1½-tonner became a major production type. In the summer of 1940 a contract went to Chevrolet for vehicles of this type which were to be based on the standard commercial model with the addition of a live front axle and transfer box to make an all-wheel-drive vehicle. As with the 2½-tonner, other military fittings were also incorporated. Chevrolet built 1½-tonners until 1945 and the grand total of vehicles completed by then was 428,196, little over half as many as the all-important 2½-tonner. Though a cargo version of the 1½-ton truck was built, this particular chassis lent itself to specialised roles and appeared with numerous bodies and fittings. Included were panel vans, airfield lighting trucks (mobile beacons), hole borer trucks for telephone poles, dumpers, crash tenders, telephone maintenance vans, and a long wheel base cargo truck. Lastly there was the type illustrated, a bomb service truck. Like many of the other types listed this was used by the U.S. Army Air Force for airfield service. This particular vehicle had an open cab and a shortened wheelbase, with single instead of dual rear wheels. The bomb lifting equipment and cradle were made by Marmon-Herrington. The gantry was designed to swing out for loading and handling bombs. The wheelbase of this vehicle was 10½ ft and it was 18½ ft long with the gantry extended. All the 1½-ton vehicles built by Chevrolet had a 93 h.p. six-cylinder engine. Other builders of 1½-ton trucks were Dodge (1940) and International (1941 onwards). These vehicles were similar in appearance to the Chevrolet but were not built as bomb service vehicles. The bomb service vehicle was used for towing bomb trolleys as well as loading bombs. Another auxiliary item used was the little Bomb Handling Trolley (Plate 97) which had a folding handle and was used for manhandling individual bombs.

98 **M20 Prime Mover, Truck, 12 ton, 6 × 4, Diamond T,** U.S.A./U.K.
99 **M9 Trailer, 40 ton, British Mk I,** 1941–45, U.K.

These two pieces of heavy equipment were intended to operate together as a Truck-Trailer combination for the recovery and transport of tanks. The Diamond T tractor was designed in 1940 to meet the requirements of the British Purchasing Mission to the U.S.A. who were placing orders with various firms to replace or supplement existing equipment. A heavy ballast body and a 20-ton power winch were standard features. The tractor had a Hercules six-cylinder diesel engine and was 23 ft 4 in. long and 8 ft 5 in. wide. The Diamond T proved to be a superb vehicle of almost unrivalled longevity. Some remained in British service in 1970—albeit re-engined with Rolls Royce motors. Late production vehicles had soft cover cabs instead of pressed steel cabs. The maximum towed load permitted was 115,000 lbs.

The M9 45-ton transporter trailer was built by Rogers Bros and was 30 ft long, with 12 wheels. The trailer's typical load was one 30-ton Sherman Tank.

This Truck-Tractor unit was originally supplied exclusively to the British, but it was subsequently used by the U.S. Army as well.

100 **Autocarro Unificato Medio, 5 ton, 4 × 2, Fiat 665,** 1940–45, Italy

The Italian Army had a less rigid system of standardisation in military transport than most other nations. Certain vehicles were adopted as 'standard' in different

load categories and the different requirements were specified. However, manufacturers did not have to comply to finely detailed specifications so there was a degree of variety in the trucks in service. The standardised medium truck (Autocarro Unificato Medio) had a payload of at least 3 tons and a speed of 60 km.p.h. while the standardised heavy truck (Autocarro Unificato Pesante) had a payload of 6 tons or more and a 45-km.p.h. speed. The Fiat 665 NL was the most modern production type in the Medio category and was based on a Fiat commercial model. With forward control and very large wheels, it had a 5-ton capacity and was a powerful and tough vehicle. Built from 1942 to 1945, it was also used in small numbers by the Germans in North Italy after Italy's capitulation. The Fiat 665 was 23 ft 3 in. long and about 8 ft 9 in. wide.

A vehicle which was of similar appearance was the Fiat 666 which was an uprated, strengthened vehicle designed to carry 6 tons and which fell into the Pesante class. The Fiat 665 had a six-cylinder diesel engine of 110 b.h.p. while the Fiat 666 had a similar engine rated at 115 b.h.p.

101 **Trattore Medio, 4 × 4, Fiat TM40,** 1940–45, Italy/Germany

Much favoured by the Italian Army was the specialised artillery tractor of compact dimensions but with big wheels and a powerful engine. First of these big wheel tractors was the Pavesi originally designed in 1914 and perfected between the wars. It is described and illustrated in the previous volume. While the Pavesi was unique in having an articulated chassis, later tractor types had a rigid wheelbase. Fiat took over Pavesi in the twenties. They built a light tractor in the late thirties, the TL37, and then a medium tractor, the TM40, in 1940. This latter vehicle is shown. It utilised the same diesel engine and cab front as the Fiat 665. The open-topped body held seats for the gun crew and there was a locker for ammunition stowage at the rear. Overall length of this vehicle was just over 15 ft.

102 **M2 Truck-mounted Crane (Thew Shovel MC 6 × 6) and M16 3-ton Trailer,** 1940–45, U.S.A.

The Thew Shovel was one of several large all-wheel drive truck-mounted cranes used by the U.S. Engineer Corps for heavy construction work. Basically this equipment consisted of a 6 × 6 chassis with platform and half-cab, carrying a complete crane housing and jib built by Lorain. The crane turntable had its own engine and the vehicle was jacked up on outriggers when operating at full capacity. Maximum lift was 40,000 lb with the boom topped up to give 11 ft radius. With the outriggers not in use, maximum lift was 21,850 lb. The Thew Shovel was normally operated with a normal purchase but it could be fitted optionally with a clamshell grab. This was transported separately in the M16 3-ton trailer (shown in the foreground) which was towed by the parent vehicle or by an accompanying truck.

The Thew Shovel was 25 ft long, excluding the crane boom. It had a Hercules HXC six-cylinder engine.

103 **M26 Truck-Tractor, 12 ton, 6 × 6, with M15 Tank Transporter Semi-Trailer,** 1943–45, U.S.A.

Pacific Car Foundry Co. made the 6 × 6 12-ton tractor which became the standard tank recovery vehicle in the U.S. Army, used together with the M15 and M15A1 Transporter Semi-Trailer. The tractor had an armoured cab with a ring mount for a ·50 calibre AA machine gun. It was powered by a 240 b.h.p. Hall Scott six-cylinder engine and had three winches, one in front with a 35,000-lb pull and two at the back of 60,000 lb each.

The M15 and M15A1 Transporters were of 40–45 tons capacity and had 8 wheels. They were made by Freuheuf the well-known trailer specialists. Both were externally similar but the M15A1 was stressed to take the heavier load.

In 1945 a new unarmoured version of the M26 Tractor appeared, designated M26A1. This had an open cab and was unarmoured both to reduce weight and because the armour was found to be of limited value in any case on the M26. The M26 was 25 ft 7 in. long, 10 ft 10½ in. wide and 10 ft 7 in. high.

104 **Lorry, 3 ton, 6 × 4, Signals Office, Austin K6,** 1942–45, U.K.
105 **Lorry, 3 ton, 6 × 4, Breakdown Gantry, Austin K6,** 1944–46, U.K.

The 3-ton 6 × 4 chassis was evolved by British manufacturers in the inter-war period to meet WD requirements and several examples are featured in the previous volume. By 1940 the simpler 3-ton 4 × 2 chassis was replacing the

6 × 4 type for general service but there remained a limited requirement for the 6 × 4 type for special purpose bodies. The principal 6 × 4 producers in the war years were Austin and Ford. In 1940 the Austin K3 (Plate 8) was in production in 6 × 4 form and in 1942 this was superseded by the K6 model which had a simplified bonnet and other detail changes. A major user of the K6 was the Royal Air Force who had vehicles in service with several types of 'house' body. These vehicles were used mainly as mobile signals and radio offices. The bodies varied in detail with regard to door and window positions but were generally as shown. This body was also used on the Ford WOT1 chassis shown in Plate 32.

The most widely used Army version of the K6 was the Breakdown Gantry model which was employed in the light recovery role. This had a braced gantry with a travelling purchase, plus a 5-ton winch fitted behind the cab between the body and the chassis. When towing or carrying a load from the rear gantry, pig iron weights were carried on the brackets across the radiator front to balance the vehicle. These Breakdown Gantry vehicles were very successful and some were still in service in 1960 and beyond. In its breakdown form the K6 was 20 ft 3 in. long and $7\frac{1}{2}$ ft wide. It had the same six-cylinder engine as other Austin trucks of the period.

106 **Lorry, 3 ton, GS, 4 × 4, Austin K5,** 1940–45, U.K.
107 **Lorry, 4 × 4, Anti-Tank Portee (6 pdr.), Austin K5,** 1940–45, U.K.

The Austin K5 was produced con-

currently with the Bedford QL (Plates 48–52), and was developed by Austin at the same time as Vauxhall were developing the Bedford. Like the Bedford it went into production in 1941 and was produced until 1945 by which time a total of 12,000 had been made. After the Bedford it was the most numerous of the British four-wheel-drive types. Except in the earliest production models the cab roof was detachable to reduce the overall height for shipping purposes.

The Austin K5 chassis also formed the basis for one of the special anti-tank gun Portee vehicles. This class of vehicle was not, in fact new, examples of World War I period Portees being shown in the previous volume. The campaign in the Western Desert in 1941–42, however, showed the need for high mobility and at the same time towed anti-tank guns proved to be exceptionally vulnerable. This was due to the lack of cover which put an emplaced gun at a disadvantage while opposing tanks were able to move swiftly due to the lack of obstacles. It was therefore decided to give maximum mobility to the anti-tank guns by reviving the old Portee idea. A Morris C8 chassis was used for the 2-pdr. anti-tank gun, but for the much heavier 6 pdr. a larger 4 × 4 chassis in the 3-ton class was found necessary. Portee versions were built of the Austin K5, the Bedford QL, and the Chevrolet CMP 3-tonner. The first two featured a flatbed body and an open half cab with a canvas top. The gun was carried on the flatbed body, on to which it was run via ramps kept under the body. The gun could be carried to fire either forward or to the rear. The nature of the vehicle was concealed from the enemy by a canvas tilt (not shown) which fitted over the framework provided. The gun could fire from the vehicle (it was known as 'Portee and Fire') or it could be towed in the normal manner. A blast shield was fitted over the vehicle's bonnet for forward firing. After the war in North Africa in 1943, the chance to use the Portee in its intended manner diminished and most Portees were later rebuilt with GS bodies.

The Austin K5 was 19 ft 8 in. long, 8½ ft wide, and had a six-cylinder petrol engine of 85 b.h.p.

108 Truck, ¼ ton, 4 × 4, Command Reconnaissance, Ford GPW in British Service as Royal Signals Line Layer, U.S.A./U.K.
109 Truck, ¼ ton, 4 × 4, Command Reconnaissance, Willys MA, U.S.A.
110 Truck, ¼ ton, 4 × 4, Utility, Willys MB with 3-litter Ambulance kit, U.S.A./U.K.
111 Truck, ¼ ton, 4 × 4, Utility, Ford GPW, converted for 'Jeep Railway', U.S.A./U.K.
112 Truck, ¼ ton, 4 × 4, Amphibian, Ford GPA, U.S.A. All 1940-45
Of all military vehicles emanating from the World War II period, the celebrated Jeep must rate as the most original and as a true milestone in automotive history. It created a new category of vehicle—the so-called 'field car'—and this found a market in the commercial world after the war so that today there are several makes of vehicle all owing something to the original Jeep design of 1940.

In the U.S. Army the Jeep fell into an additional load category, ¼ ton, which had not been allowed for when the original five basic classes of military vehicle were worked out.

Ideas for a military light reconnais-sance car were first put forward in the late 1930s and in summer 1940 the Bantam Car Co. designed and made a prototype to meet U.S. Army requirements. Bantam marketed Austin 7 cars in America and used some ideas (and components) for their prototype from the well-known 'baby' Austin. The Bantam field car was a plain open-topped vehicle and 70 examples were purchased by the U.S. Ordnance Department for testing. Trials were impressive and the Ordnance Department were anxious to order another 1,500 vehicles. Their request to do so, however, was blocked by the Quartermaster-General on the grounds that Bantam themselves had severely limited production facilities and would be unable to fulfill the order.

Meanwhile two other firms, Willys-Overland and Ford, were also building prototypes to meet the Army requirement. At the time the Bantam cab was tested neither Willy's nor Ford had completed their vehicles. However, in November 1940 all three firms received contracts for 1,500 vehicles even though the Willys and Ford prototypes were still not built. The premature award of contracts, however, before prototypes were seen caused annoyance to Bantam and other sections of industry.

The Willys and Ford prototypes were eventually finished in November and December 1940, when all three vehicles were then tested together. All had minor detail faults and structural weaknesses but the Willys design was eventually judged the winner and this firm received the production contract. Bantam were excluded due to their limited production capacity, an ironic fate for the firm which did so much pioneering work on the original design.

The first order for 16,000 vehicles was placed immediately and the first production vehicle appeared in December 1941. With increased orders, however, Willys could not keep pace with demand and Ford were thus brought in to build vehicles to the Willys pattern. By the end of the war a total of 639,245 of what were subsequently called Jeeps had been built. There were several different production models which are identified as follows:

Willys MA: the 1500 vehicles built to the original Willys design for the original contract. Headlamps atop mudguards (Plate 109).

Ford GP: the 1500 vehicles built to the original Ford design. Rounded mudguards at front.

Willys MB: Main production type —squared off front mudguard. (Plate 110.)

Ford GPW: Built by Ford to Willys design and identical to the Willys MB in all but minor details. (Plate 111.)

The early MA and GP models, though not of the finalised designs, did nonetheless see service, mainly under Lend-Lease when many were supplied to Britain and Russia.

In service the Jeep became a legend for the many roles in which it was employed. Just a few of these are illustrated here. Plate 108 shows a Ford GPW model converted to a Royal Signals linelayer and used in the airborne role. The Jeep could be carried in the RAF Horsa glider (background) and became the main transport vehicle for airborne units. The American Hadrian glider could also carry a Jeep.

Jeeps were used extensively as front line ambulances (Plate 110) with kits of parts to enable a quick conversion in the field. A three-litter version is shown but there were also two- and four-litter variants, the latter having a high canvas tilt and carrying the stretchers in two layers. Plate 111 shows a Jeep railway such as was used in several theatres of war. The wheels were replaced by flanged wheels and the vehicle became a self-contained 'locomotive' which could haul trailers along the track. They were widely used in the Far East. A homemade condenser to conserve the cooling water is added to the vehicle drawn.

Other special conversions of Jeeps included the heavily armed vehicles used by the Special Air Service and similar clandestine forces, Jeep cranes, traffic control vehicles, and many others. The Jeep could also mount a recoilless rifle or tow the 6-pdr. anti-tank gun, a 75-mm pack howitzer, or a $\frac{1}{2}$-ton cargo trailer.

The Amphibious Jeep (Plate 112) was based on the standard Jeep chassis and engine but had a boat-like body designed by a naval architect firm, Sparkman and Stephen of New York. The overall design was by Marmon Herrington. Water propulsion was by a propeller driven by a power take off from the transmission. An anchor was a standard fitting and this vehicle was designated Ford GPA.

The Jeep took its name from its designation GP. This name had originally been similarly used with the Dodge $\frac{1}{2}$-ton truck and the $\frac{1}{4}$-ton truck was to be called the Peep, reflecting its reconnaissance role. However, somehow this never caught on and Jeep became the familiar name for the $\frac{1}{4}$-tonner—so familiar in fact that the name was later registered as a trademark by Willys-Overland, the vehicle's builders. The original designation 'Command Reconnaissance' was later changed to 'Utility' when it became apparent that this handy little vehicle had many more uses than were originally envisaged.

The standard Jeep had a 54 b.h.p. four-cylinder in-line engine with six forward speeds and two reverse. It was 11 ft long, 5 ft 2 in. wide, and 6 ft high with the canvas hood erected. It was only $4\frac{1}{4}$ ft high with the hood and windscreen lowered, however. The wheelbase was 6 ft 8 in.

113 Lorry, 3 ton, 4 × 4, Breakdown Gantry, Ford WOT6, 1940–45, U.K.

Ford of Britain were another firm asked to produce 4 × 4 trucks to the same WD specification as Vauxhall (Bedford) and Austin. After these two, the Ford vehicle was the next most numerous. It entered production later than the others, in early 1942 and was built until late 1945. It utilised the well-known Ford V-8 engine which gave 85 b.h.p. In its GS cargo truck form it was 19 ft $10\frac{1}{2}$ in. long and was $7\frac{1}{2}$ ft wide. Several specialist bodies were fitted to this chassis including the Breakdown Gantry (illustrated) and Machinery and Repair. These Fords proved very reliable and a few remained in military service as recently as 1962.

114 Artillery Tractor S-80, 1940–45, U.S.S.R.

The Soviet Army made wide use of fully-tracked agricultural type tractors for much of their artillery haulage during World War II. While by contemporary Western standards this was a slow and primitive method of moving guns, the Russian automotive industry lagged behind the West in 1940 and trucks suitable for use as medium or heavy artillery tractors were in short supply. On the other hand there was a big tractor industry resulting from the pre-war Five Year Plans which had concentrated on tractors for farming. In the conditions of snow, slush, and mud which prevailed in Russia for a good part of the year, fully-tracked tractors were in fact at an advantage as roads were often impassible to wheeled transport—as the Germans found to their cost in the successive winter campaigns on the Russian Front.

Two very similar agricultural tractors which saw military service in large numbers were the S-65 and S-80 Stalinets which were six-cylinder diesel vehicles of conventional tractor layout. The later S-80 (the version shown) remained in military service for about 10 years after the end of the war. The suspension was copied from the American Holt type. A prominent winch was mounted on the rear platform behind the enclosed cab.

During World War II, apart from indigenous GAZ and ZIS trucks (see previous volume) Soviet Russia was dependent on Lend-Lease supplies from America for the bulk of her motor transport. The $2\frac{1}{2}$-tonner, Jeep, DUKW, and $\frac{3}{4}$-ton trucks shown in this book were all supplied to Russia in vast numbers in the years 1942–45.

115 **Lorry, 3 ton, 4 × 2, Petrol Carrier, Dennis**
116 **Lorry, 3 ton, 4 × 2, Tipping, Dennis,** 1940–45, U.K.

Dennis produced a number of 3-ton 4 × 2 types for the British Army which were not used in forward areas like 4 × 4 types but which nonetheless gave good service in the hands of the various support services. The Dennis 3-tonner was virtually identical to the commercial truck which Dennis were selling in 1939. Two of the most widely used variants were the end tipper (Plate 116) and the petrol tanker (Plate 115). The tipper had a wood dropside body and hydraulic tipping mechanism. It was widely used by the Royal Engineers and some were also used by the Royal Air Force in airfield construction and repair work. The petrol tanker was, again, essentially the commercial model and was used mainly by the Royal Army Service Corps at bases in England.

These Dennis vehicles had a four-cylinder 75 b.h.p. engine and the tipper variant was 17 ft 9 in. long.

117 **M5, 13 ton, High-Speed Tractor,** 1940–45, U.S.A.

Once the American re-armament programme was under way in 1941, the Army decided as a longer term policy to switch wholly to tracked transport for all except supply and liaison vehicles in armoured divisions. This meant that wheeled and half-track gun tractors would be replaced by fully tracked tractors. A whole family of purpose-built tractor designs was put in hand. In passing it must be noted that the scheme to have tracked vehicles only was never

fully implemented because demand always outstripped supply. Thus wheeled and half-track gun tractors and carriers were still in service at the end of the war.

To tow the 105-mm and 155-mm field howitzers a vehicle originally designated T21 Medium Tractor was developed by International Harvester Co., the prototype being ready late in 1941. The tracks and suspension were based on those of the M3 Light Tank (an alternative design with rubber tracks was rejected by the Army). The new vehicle was standardised as the M5 Medium Tractor in October 1942 when it entered service. Later it was called by its final title of High-Speed Tractor. The M5 proved to be a most successful design and saw wide service. It weighed 28,000 lbs, was 15 ft 11 in. long, 8 ft 4 in. wide, and 8 ft 8 in. high. It had a crew of 9 and a Continental R-6522 235 h.p. air-cooled engine which gave it a speed of 35 m.p.h. A winch was mounted on the front and air brakes were included for operating the brakes on the gun being towed.

118 **M4, 18 ton, High-Speed Tractor,** 1940–45, U.S.A.

This was a complementary vehicle to the M5 Tractor designed to tow the 155-mm gun, 240-mm howitzer or the 90-mm AA gun (or equivalent equipment up to 30,000 lbs). The vehicle was developed and built by Allis-Chalmers using chassis components from the M2A1 Medium Tank. Those vehicles equipped to tow the 90-mm AA gun had different ammunition stowage arrangements compared to the other vehicles which had a folding ammunition hoist not fitted to the AA gun tractors. The M4 (originally T9 Medium Tractor) was comfortably equipped and had full weather protection. It was powered by a Waukesha 145G2 210 h.p. engine which gave a top tow speed of 33 m.p.h. It weighed 31,500 lbs, was 16 ft 11 in. long, 7 ft 10 in. high, and 8 ft 1 in. wide. There was accommodation for an 11-man gun crew. A 0·50 calibre Browning machine gun could be mounted on the cab roof for local AA defence. This vehicle entered production in late 1942 and was in wide service by 1944.

119 M6, 38 ton, High-Speed Tractor, 1940–45, U.S.A.

Largest of the High Speed Tractor family was the M6, also built by Allis-Chalmers. This was essentially an enlarged version of the M4 Tractor and was intended to tow the 240-mm gun or loads of up to 50,000 lbs. It had twin Waukesha six-cylinder engines, giving twice the power of the M4 Tractor. Total weight of the vehicle was 76,000 lbs and it was 21½ ft long and 10 ft wide. This vehicle had Allis-Chalmers own design of scissors suspension and did not use parts from other vehicles. Air and electric brake pipes were fitted for controlling the tow, and there was a 30-ton winch. A Browning ·5-calibre machine gun could be fitted in the commander's roof hatch. There was accommodation for a gun crew of 10 men.

120 Truck, ¾ ton, 4 × 4, Command Car, Dodge
121 Truck, ¾ ton, 4 × 4, Command Reconnaissance Car, Dodge, 1940–45, U.S.A.

With the standardisation of the ¼-ton Jeep the U.S. Army decided to upgrade their previous smallest category of truck from ½ ton to ¾ ton. Ford and Dodge (the previous main builders of ½-tonners) each produced prototype vehicles for evaluation and these new designs closely followed the lines of the Jeep. Compared to the ½-ton vehicles they were slightly wider and lower and had bigger wheels and tyres and stronger springs. The Dodge design was chosen for production and the new category of truck was officially introduced in June 1942 when production got under way. The ¾-ton truck series eventually supplanted the ½-tonners and remained in service for many years after the war.

As with the ½-ton series there were several special body types. The most common variant was the Command Reconnaissance Car (Plate 121) which was used for liaison work and as senior officers' transport in virtually all fighting units. It was fitted with seats and mapboards and had a detachable canvas top and sidescreens. This was produced both with and without a winch. Another variant, the Command Car (or 'Command Field Sedan') was produced in smaller numbers for staff officers and formation commanders (Plate 120). This was an elaborately equipped vehicle based on panel van type bodywork. Side doors were added together with map table, radio and roof rack. Blackout blinds were fitted in the rear windows so that the vehicle could be used as a mobile headquarters at any time.

Another version utilising the same body was the Carryall, which lacked the side doors and fittings, and was used as a runabout.

Other models on the ¾-ton chassis were the Weapons Carrier, Ambulance, Radio Truck, and various Repair Trucks.

Of these the most widely used was the Weapons Carrier which had an open body with personnel seats, a canvas tilt and canvas side screens. This was sometimes called the 'Beep'—perhaps a corruption of 'Big Jeep'. One further variant was the M6 Gun Motor Carriage which in essence was a Weapons Carrier mounting a 37-mm anti-tank gun in the rear compartment. This saw limited service in Europe in 1944–45.

The Dodge $\frac{3}{4}$-ton vehicles were powered by a six-cylinder 92 b.h.p. engine and in Command Reconnaissance form the vehicle was 14 ft long and $6\frac{1}{2}$ ft wide. It weighed 5,375 lbs.

122 Landing Vehicle Tracked, Armoured, Mk 4—LVT 4, 1943–45, U.S.A./U.K.

What later became known variously as the Alligator or Water Buffalo and was produced in several forms was originated in 1935 when an engineer called Donald Roebling Jnr produced a light tracked amphibious vehicle for rescue work in the swamps of the Florida Everglades. The United States Marine Corps became interested and in 1940 Roebling redesigned his vehicle to meet their requirements. This went into production in 1941 as the LVT1. A succeeding model was the LVT(A)1, which was made of armour plate and mounted a turret to form what was virtually an amphibious tank. The LVT2 and LVT(A)2 were improved versions of the original design, basically a boat-shaped tracked hull with engine compartment aft, cab forward, and a load space in the middle. This design had a disadvantage in that only personnel and light stores could be carried and men and equipment had to embark and disembark over the sides of the vehicle rather in the manner of boarding a boat. Under amphibious landing conditions this exposed the men to gunfire, so a complete redesign was carried out. In this the engine was moved forward to behind the front crew cab. The transom was then replaced by a hinged ramp operated by a hand winch. Stores and men could then enter and leave the vehicle at the back, protected from ground fire to some extent by the bulk of the vehicle. Designated LVT4 and called the Buffalo by the British, this vehicle could carry up to 30 men and/or light vehicles and guns. A typical load would be a jeep, a Universal Carrier, or a 6-pdr. gun.

The LVT 4 was a most successful design which was used in large numbers by the Americans (both Army and Marines) in the Pacific, and was used by both the British and Americans in Italy and Europe in 1943–45. Buffaloes figured prominently in the Rhine crossing and the Walcheren landings, playing a key part in the success of those operations.

The vehicle propelled itself in the water by the cup-shaped grousers on its tracks. The drawing shows the ramp arrangement. The Buffalo was normally armed for self-defence only with a ·30 or ·50 calibre machine gun in a pintle mount each side. Some vehicles had a prominent shield for each gun. Vehicles in British service also had a 20-mm Polsten cannon mounted atop the cab and firing forward. A few British vehicles carried flame throwers as well.

The LVT4 was 26 ft 1 in. long, 8 ft 1 in. high, and 10 ft 8 in. wide. It had a Continental W-670 engine of 250 h.p. and had a top speed of 25 m.p.h. on land and $6\frac{1}{2}$ m.p.h. in water. It had a crew of three.

123 **M29 Cargo Carrier, Weasel,**
1942–45 U.S.A./U.K.
124 **M29C Cargo Carrier, Amphibious, Weasel,** 1943–45, U.S.A./U.K.

The Weasel was a light tracked vehicle originally designed with winter warfare and transportation in mind. It had wide rubber tracks and was lightly constructed, weighing only 2 tons. It was designed and built by the Studebaker Corporation and had a Studebaker six-cylinder engine. It proved a most excellent design and saw wide post-war service, particularly with the Canadian and Norwegian Armies who operate extensively under winter conditions. Some Weasels were still in service in 1970.

The amphibious model M29C had a new flotation body, boat-shaped front and rear, and with cable-operated rudders at the rear. Propulsion in the water was achieved by movement of the tracks. The amphibious version of the Weasel was supplied to the British Army in 1944 and was used as a support vehicle in various amphibious operations in Europe such as the Walcheren landings. It was 16 ft long, 6½ ft wide, and 6 ft high with the canvas cover erected. The non-amphibious model was 10½ ft long, lacking as it did the flotation chambers at each end.

125 **Kfz 31 Krankenkraftwagen (4 × 4, Phänomen Granit 1500A)**
126 **Schwerer Personenkraftwagen (4 × 4, Phänomen Granit 1500A),** 1940–45, Germany

The smallest standardised class under the German Schell Programme was the

1½-tonner. Phänomen Granit, Steyr, Mercedes Benz and Auto-Union all built trucks in this range. As before they were made as Type A (4 × 4) or Type B (4 × 2), Type A being purely for military use. A range of bodywork which included ambulance (Plate 125), Kubelwagen (personnel carrier) (Plate 126) and cargo truck could be seen on the Phänomen Granit 1500A chassis. The standard 'house' body was used for the ambulance and there were some stores, maintenance, and command vehicles all with the same body. The Phänomen-Granit had an air-cooled four-cylinder diesel engine and was 14¾ ft long in its personnel carrier form. For desert operations an extra air filter was carried on the bonnet of the personnel carrier.

127 **Truck, Amphibious, 2½ ton, 6 × 6, DUKW,** 1942–45, U.S.A./U.K.
128 **Truck, Amphibious, 2½ ton, 6 × 6, DUKW with Experimental Mat-laying Equipment,** 1944–45, U.S.A.

A major new project in 1942 was the attempt to produce a vehicle which could be used to unload ships and landing craft by transhipping stores over open beaches without the benefit of prepared harbours. This was foreseen as just one of the requirements for planned future Allied landings in Europe and Italy. The National Defense Research Committee were given the task of organising this project, though neither the U.S. Navy nor the Army were keen on the possible complications of the idea. However, the NDRC engaged the services of naval architects Sparkman and Stephens of New York (they also designed the

Amphibious Jeep) who worked with Yellow Truck and Coach Co.—main builders of the 2½-ton truck—to produce a boat-shaped flotation hull to fit the standard COE type 2½-ton 6 × 6 chassis (as shown in Plate 92). From the builders code for the vehicle—DUKW—the conveniently amphibious name 'Duck' was contrived. (D = 1942; U = utility; K = all wheel drive; W = twin rear wheel axles.)

On land the DUKW used its normal style of drive but in the water it was propelled by a propeller (on a power take-off from the transmission) and steered by a rudder. Wheels and propeller could operate together for entering or leaving the water. The pilot model DUKW was so successful that it was put into production at once and was first used at the landings in Noumea in March 1943. Shortly after that DUKW were used in the invasion of Sicily and from then on they were used in all amphibious operations. In 1943, 4,508 vehicles were built and by late 1945 when production ceased, 21,247 were built. DUKWs saw service for many years after the war and some remained in service with British and other armies as late as 1970. DUKWs carried anchors and other nautical fittings.

The drawings show the optional AA machine gun mount and the rear channel for the propeller and rudders. Plate 128 shows a U.S. Marines experimental version designed to lay a wire grid mat over soft sand so that trucks leaving a landing craft had a ready made 'road' to follow which avoided the risk of bogging down. Steel runners and a stowage bin for mat are the additions made to the main structure for this role. The British used a similar device fitted to a Buffalo.

156

The DUKW was 36 ft long and 8 ft wide. It could carry 59 men or the equivalent weight in stores. DUKWs were supplied to Soviet Russia under Lend-Lease and the Russians built a pirated copy known as the ZIL-485. This differed from the American original in having the cargo space extended to the rear and a rear loading ramp.

129 **Schwerer Gelandegangiger Lastkraftwagen offen (4 × 4, Mercedes Benz L4500A, A Type),** 1941–45, Germany

This was a further heavy type of truck produced in Germany under the Schell Programme (see Plates 57–61). Vehicles in this type first appeared under the Schell Programme for none in this load class (3½–5 tons) had been used by the Wehrmacht before. Comparison with Plates 60 and 61 will show how rigid the Schell Programme specifications were, for these vehicles all look identical except for differing cabs and bonnets. The A Type had four-wheel-drive but Mercedes Benz also produced an S Type version in 4 × 2 form. This looked very similar except that it lacked a driven front axle and was in consequence slightly lower in height. There was also a self-propelled gun version made in small numbers. This had a 37-mm Flak gun mounted on a flat bed body, and an enclosed armoured cab. Overall length of this vehicle was 22½ ft. It had a six-cylinder diesel engine giving 112 b.h.p.

130 **GAZ-67B Field Car,** 1943–53, U.S.S.R.

The Russian equivalent to the Jeep was

obviously inspired by this vehicle, or more probably the Bantam of which many of the 1,500 production batch (see Plate 109) were supplied under Lend-Lease. The body and headlamp arrangement more closely followed the Bantam than the Jeep proper. This Russian vehicle utilised the Soviet-built four-cylinder Ford Model A engine (the pre-war Russian motor industry was largely based on Ford products built under licence—see previous volume). The wheels, suspension and many components were similar to those used on the GAZ cars, but four-wheel-drive was introduced. The fuel tank was under the scuttle. The vehicle was used for the same variety of roles as the Jeep, and in fact the Russians used thousands of Jeeps too. Production of the GAZ-67B did not cease until 1963 and many are still in service with Russian satellite nations.

131   Ostradschlepper (4 × 4, Skoda 175), 1942–44, Germany

The name Ostradschlepper (East-wheeled-tractor) succinctly describes this most unusual vehicle which was specially designed as an artillery tractor for use on the Russian (or Eastern) Front. It was thought that large wheels were the answer to the difficult problem of handling wheeled transport in the severe snow and mud encountered in Russia. To the Germans the weather was often a greater menace than Russian troops and many measures were tried in an attempt to alleviate the problems which winter brought.

Dr. Ferdinand Porsche, brilliant designer of the Volkswagen car and very active in the field of tank design, was responsible for designing this new vehicle and 200 were built by the Czech firm of Skoda in 1942. They had 80-h.p. four-cylinder diesel engines and were 18 ft long, 7½ ft wide, and 9 ft 1½ in. high. A few vehicles had petrol engines. These Ostradschleppers were used until the end of the war but they offered no great advance over conventional tractors and were less easy to handle. The vehicle drawn is displaying the German national flag as an air recognition sign to friendly aircraft.

132   Raupenschlepper-Ost (Steyr RSO/01)
133   Raupenschlepper-Ost (Steyr RSO/03), 1942–45, Germany

Another attempt to produce vehicles specially suited to winter conditions on the Eastern Front resulted in the fully-tracked Raupenschlepper-Ost (tracked tractor-East). This vehicle was originally built by Steyr (RSO/01) (Plate 132) and had a pressed steel truck type cab and COE layout. It was powered by a Steyr V-8 70-b.h.p. engine. It had tank-like torsion bar suspension and steel tracks. Special wide (600 mm) tracks were fitted for running on snow or slush though conventional narrow (340 mm) tracks were normally fitted. The vehicle was rated at 1½-tons capacity. It was 14½ ft long, 6·57 ft wide, and 8·2 ft high. An improved model, the RSO/03 (Plate 133), was built by Magirus in 1944 and was simplified with a plain squared-off open cab and canvas top. This vehicle had a Deutz four-cylinder diesel engine but in other respects was similar to the RSO/01. This particular model also formed the basis of a light self-propelled mount for a 7·5-cm Pak gun; 83 vehicles were so converted. In the last year of the war the Radschlepper-Ost was also used in small numbers on the Western Front.

134 Tractor, 20 ton, 6 × 6, Scammell Constructor
135 Vickers-Vigo Tractor/Dozer on 20-ton Low-loading Machinery Trailer, 1953, U.K.

One of the first of several new Scammell designs to come into service with the post-war British Army, the 20-ton 6 × 6 Tractor, was designed expressly for towing the 20-ton low-loading Machinery Trailer which was mainly used for transporting Royal Engineers plant and equipment. The Scammell— known as the Constructor to its makers —had a ballast body which also included space for recovery equipment and spare wheels. The vehicle had towing pintles fore and aft and featured a chassis-mounted winch rated at 15 tons which could be led forward or aft. The tractor was 23 ft 8 in. long, 10 ft high, and 8 ft 8 in. wide. Its total weight was 59,360 lbs fully loaded. Power was from a Scammell-Meadows six-cylinder petrol engine giving 181 b.h.p. Governed top speed was 28 m.p.h. This type of vehicle was still in service in 1970 though partly supplanted by a later model (see Plate 177).

The 20-ton eight-wheel low-loading Machinery Trailer is in general service for carrying engineers' plant and other bulky equipment. The rear axles and wheels are removable for loading and two loading ramps provided are carried on the deck. Overall length is 30 ft 9 in. and the width is 8½ ft. This type of trailer is still in service.

The typical load shown is a Vickers-Vigo Tractor/Dozer, a widely used Royal Engineers' type with a high capacity dozer blade.

136 Truck, 4 × 4, 10 ton, Scammell Mountaineer, 1955, U.K.

This is virtually a 4 × 4 version of the 20-ton tractor (Plate 134). It was not produced for the British Army but has been sold overseas to smaller forces requiring a versatile heavy general service vehicle. The flat bed and stake body shown is an alternative to a cargo body. The vehicle is winch-fitted, and optional engines can be fitted to suit the user's needs.

137 Tractor, 10 ton, 6 × 6, GS Recovery, Scammell, 1953, U.K.

Built as a replacement for the wartime Scammell heavy breakdown tractor (Plate 78), this vehicle is intended for the recovery of vehicles (e.g. trucks and armoured cars) up to 10 tons in weight. The major change is the addition of a driven front axle but otherwise this vehicle closely resembles its forerunner. It has a powered jib winch and a main winch in the chassis rated at 15 tons. The engine is a Scammell/Meadows six-cylinder petrol unit rated at 181 b.h.p. Overall length is 20 ft 7½ in., width 8½ ft, and height 10 ft 4½ in. This vehicle was still in service in 1970 though partly supplanted by a later design.

138 Truck, 7½ ton, 6 × 6, Prime Mover, Mack NO, 1941–45, U.S.A.

The Mack NO series was the major wheeled gun tractor built for the U.S.

Army during World War II and was intended as a tractor for the 155-mm gun. It was a conventional 'heavy-heavy' class vehicle of 6 × 6 configuration, fitted with a winch at the front. It had a Mack EY six-cylinder engine of 159 b.h.p. and was 24 ft 9 in. long and 8 ft 9 in. wide. It had an unusual arrangement for the front driven axle in that the usual universal joint was dispensed with in favour of a bevelled double gear reduction in the axle ends which allowed for both drive and steering. The Mack NO series of successively improved models were supplied to other nations using the 155-mm gun. The British Army was still using these vehicles in 1970. A distinctive feature is a yoke attached to the rear of the chassis and body which carries a chain purchase to lift the heavy trail of the gun when attaching the limber wheels for towing.

139 Truck, ¾ ton, 4 × 4, Weapons Carrier, Dodge, 1943–50, U.S.A.

This was the Weapons Carrier model of the Dodge ¾-ton series described in Plates 120 and 121. The drawing shows the winch-fitted model which was 14 ft 8½ in. long. The Weapons Carrier version was produced in far greater numbers than the special bodied variants and remained in service for many years postwar before being replaced by a similar but improved model. The Weapons Carrier was also built by Dodge in Canada and this type of vehicle was supplied under Lend-Lease to several nations. The type is still used by several small nations within the American sphere of influence.

140 Truck, 4 ton, 6 × 6, Van, Diamond T
141 Truck, 4 ton, 6 × 6, Dumper, Diamond T, 1941–45, U.S.A.

In the 1940–41 period the main emphasis in new truck procurement concentrated on the 2½, ½, and ¼-ton types. These were the main vehicles needed for tactical use, i.e., in direct support of front line units. Only a few hundred larger vehicles were ordered at this time. Among these were Diamond Ts and various other makes. In June 1942 when the various categories of truck were standardised and the designs 'frozen', the Diamond T was selected as the 4-ton 6 × 6 type for future production, other makes in this class being then dropped. By this time the lighter trucks had all been in production for from one to two years and manufacturing facilities were well established. The production of heavier trucks—4 tons and above were called 'heavy-heavy' trucks—was undertaken by specialist firms whose facilities were less extensive than the mass-producers like Ford and GMC who were building the lighter classes of vehicle. Hence there was a serious shortage of 'heavy-heavy' trucks in 1943–44 when the Army suddenly realised from experience in North Africa and Italy that it had insufficient trucks to maintain its lengthening supply routes in these areas. The demand for twice as many 'heavy-heavy' trucks—with a production target raised from 3,000 a month to 6,000—was never completely satisfied nor, indeed, was it reached very often. However, by rationalising component production, utilising spare capacity in other plants, and by a top priority production scheme, the 6,000 target was

159

handsomely exceeded by December, 1944. Meanwhile the invasion of North-West Europe had increased the demand for trucks even more and maximum utilisation of existing trucks was necessary. This led to the 'Red Ball Highway Express' route and other routes in other theatres which were extensively worked and well policed and protected to keep the traffic moving.

The Diamond T 4-tonner had the standard U.S. Army pattern cargo body, but the illustrations show two specialist bodies on the 4-ton chassis. The van body (Plate 140) was used for various roles including workshop, repair, machinery, and printing (differing in internal fittings, of course). The dumper body (Plate 141) was more widely built and was used mainly by the Engineers Corps. It had a hydraulic upper mechanism. The Diamond T (cargo version) was 22 ft 4½ in. long, 8 ft wide, and 9 ft 10½ in. high. It had a Hercules RXC six-cylinder engine of 106 b.h.p. Weight was 18,050 lbs. Late production vehicles had open cabs and a canvas roof and sidescreens.

142 **Amphibious Personnel Carrier K-61,** 1952, U.S.S.R.

Like the Western powers, the Russians learned the value of amphibious vehicles as a result of the campaigns of World War II. During the war the Red Army was very short of any kind of amphibious vehicle and river crossings became lengthy and hazardous operations as a result. After the war the Russians provided 'snorting' gear for their tanks (allowing deep-submerged-wading) and a whole range of amphibious vehicles was produced. The first of these was a Russian-built copy of the DUKW

and the second was the K-61 tracked amphibious carrier which entered service in the early 1950s. This vehicle was a very close copy of a little-used German World War II vehicle, the Land-Wasserschlepper. This had been designed in the 1943–45 period as an assault engineer vehicle to afford speedy crossings of rivers. The K-61 reproduced all the essential features of the Land-Wasserschlepper and was almost the same dimensionally except for its increased length. The mode of propulsion —twin propellers in recessed channels, each with its own rudder—was identical as was the lower hull shape. The track pattern and layout was also similar but used Russian components. The rest of the hull, however, differed completely from the Land-Wasserschlepper. It was open topped and had a loading ramp at the stern as also featured in the Russian-made DUKW. This facilitated loading of men or stores straight off the adjacent river bank.

The K-61 was not armoured, having a pressed steel lightweight flotation body. It had a crew of 3 and could carry 32 troops or the equivalent weight in stores. It weighed 9½ tons and had a 130-h.p. diesel engine. Top land speed was 36 km.p.h. snd in the water it went at 10 km.p.h. Overall length was 29·7 ft, width was just over 10 ft, and the height was 6·8 ft.

143 **LKW, 10 ton, 6 × 6, Faun 908/54VA**
144 **LKW, 10 ton, 6 × 6, Faun L912/21HOH**
145 **LKW, 12 ton, 6 × 6, Faun L912/45A,** 1958, Federal Germany

When the Federal German Army (Bundeswehr) was formed in the 1950s it was initially equipped with mainly American equipment. However, Germany's automotive industry was well able to meet all motor transport needs. Standard classes were $\frac{1}{4}$ ton, $\frac{3}{4}$ ton, $1\frac{1}{2}$ ton, 3 ton, 5 ton and 10–12 ton. In general different manufacturers supplied vehicles in these individual classes, and the makers of the 10–12-ton range (and a few even bigger types) were Faun. These vehicles were supplied with forward control or normal control depending on function, while mechanical and chassis components were standardised throughout. Three Typical models from the range (LKW = Lastkraftwagen = motor truck) are shown here.

The model 908/54VA (Plate 143) is one of several types built on a long wheelbase 6 × 6 chassis. The version shown is a cargo/personnel carrier which has folding seats on the body side in the conventional fashion. It has an eight-cylinder Deutz engine of 178 b.h.p., a 10-ton payload capacity, and a gross weight of 22 tons. Overall length is 30·8 ft, width 7·9 ft, and height 8·8 ft. Other versions on this chassis include a bridging crane (similar in layout to the vehicle shown in Plate 146), a petrol tanker, and flatbed container carrier.

The model L912/45A (Plate 145) is representative of the short wheelbase normal control models. Rated at 12 tons it has a twelve-cylinder diesel engine of 265 b.h.p. giving a top speed of 77 km.p.h. It is 24.3 ft long, 7·9 ft wide, and 8.8 ft high. This vehicle is used as a medium artillery tractor or general cargo truck. There is also a recovery/breakdown version with a crane.

The Faun L912/21 HOH (Plate 144) (HOH = hohlplatten = ramp carrier) is a 1964–65 model on a modified version of the 12-ton chassis, using the same twelve-cylinder engine. It carries five ramp or deck sections from the standard Bundeswehr pontoon bridging range. A hydraulic tipping load platform is incorporated to facilitate unloading. Top speed of the vehicle is 64 km.p.h. and it is 29·4 ft long overall.

146   Truck, 10 ton, 6 × 6, Bridging Crane, AEC Militant, 1959, U.K.

In the middle 1950s new 10-ton vehicles were ordered by the British Army to replace vehicles of this class which had been in service since World War II. Leyland, Thorneycroft and AEC were the main suppliers, the latter firm's 6 × 6 10-tonner being known as the Militant. Versions of the Militant in service include cargo, flatbed with pallet load systems with Atlas hydraulic crane, a 2,500 gallon fuel tanker, a three-way tipper, a tractor for a 10-ton semi-trailer, and a tractor for AA guns. All these versions have a 7-ton chassis-mounted winch and a standard cab. The most distinctive vehicle in the Militant range, however, is the Bridging Crane, used by the Royal Engineers for site work in bridge-building operations or by the Ordnance Corps for equipment handling. This vehicle has a complete Coles 6-ton (shown) or Jones 6-ton crane and cab unit mounted on the chassis rear. To stow the long arm of the crane jib it was necessary to modify the cab, splitting it almost in two and providing a cradle forward of the radiator. Basic vehicle (less the crane) is 30 ft long, 8 ft 2 in. wide, and 11 ft 10 in. high. Top speed is 24 m.p.h.

147 **Light Wheeled Loader, Michigan 75 DS Mk I,** 1960, U.S.A./ U.K.

The Michigan is one of several types of earth-moving and constructional equipment used by the Royal Engineers. It can carry either a fork lift attachment (illustrated) or a shovel on its lifting arms, while a third option is a Saro portable roadway which can be carried and laid from special yoke and frame attached to the lifting arm. With this particular piece of equipment Michigans are used in amphibious landing operations where they lay trackways up the beach for the benefit of wheeled vehicles coming ashore from landing craft. Another piece of equipment used with the Michigan is a back hoe which can be attached to the rear end of the tractor when required. This is a completely self-contained item with separate operator's seat and controls, and its own hydraulics. A detachable foul weather cab is supplied with the Michigan but under operational conditions it is usually omitted. The later Mk II model of this vehicle differs principally in having exhaust outlets led vertically from the top of the hood and a filtered air intake in the same position. With these changes, plus full waterproofing the vehicle is able to operate and wade in shallow water, for instance in amphibious operations.

148 **Articulated Wheel Loader, Allis-Chalmers 645,** 1965, U.K.

Intended for field use by the Royal Engineers, the Allis-Chalmers 645 was designed as a high capacity dumper but it has a secondary function as a scraper for which a special tow hook is provided

162

to take the scraper blade. It can also be used as a tractor for light trailers. A long wheelbase in relation to its length allows the vehicle front end (the leading bogie and bucket) to be turned through 90°–45° each side of the centre line—with no loss of stability. This greatly facilitates loading and manoeuvring. The turning circle is only 17 ft 8½ in. The Allis-Chalmers 645 has a six-cylinder AEC diesel engine, dual braking (air and hydraulic with lines for trailers), and an extensive hydraulic system for operating the bucket. Overall length of the vehicle is 24 ft 4 in., width 8 ft 10 in., and height (to cab top) of 10 ft 10 in.

149 **Tractor, 10 ton, GS, 6 × 6, Medium Artillery, Leyland**
150 **Tractor, 10 ton, Leyland with Bofors Light AA gun,** 1955, U.K.

The Leyland 10-tonner was developed to replace the early types of medium artillery tractor like the Matador and the Albion (plates 3 and 76). Considerably more attention was given to crew comfort in this vehicle than in previous types. A steel body includes a cab section for 12 men while ammunition and battery stores are carried in a separate rear compartment which has a 4½-ton capacity. A 10-ton winch is fitted in the chassis, leading fore and aft, and with a 350-ft lead. Towing pintles are provided at each end as are air brake lines. There is also a lead for electric breaking if needed. This vehicle entered service in the early 1950s and remains in use, and there is a recovery vehicle on the same chassis. In gun tractor form the Leyland is 26 ft 10¼ in. long, 10 ft 1 in. high, and 8½ ft wide. It has a Rolls-Royce B series eight-cylinder engine of 215 b.h.p. (gross). Top road speed is 26 m.p.h.

Originally the Leyland tractor was used to tow 7·2 in.-guns and 5·5 in.-howitzers but with the disappearance of the former weapon from service the Leylands replaced AEC Matadors as towing vehicles for the Bofors 40 mm L.43-light anti-aircraft gun and its associated radar control unit and generator trailers. Plate 150 shows a tractor with the Bofors L.43 gun in travelling position.

151 **Truck, GS, $\frac{1}{4}$ ton, 4 × 4, Rover 8 (Land Rover) with M40A1, 106 mm Recoilless Rifle,** 1960, U.K./Australia

152 **Truck, GS, $\frac{3}{4}$ ton, 4 × 4, Rover 9 (Land Rover) with Wombat Anti-tank Gun,** 1964, U.K.

153 **Truck, GS, Utility, $\frac{1}{2}$ ton, 4 × 4, Land Rover,** 1960, U.K.

154 **Ambulance, 2–4 Stretcher, $\frac{3}{4}$ ton, 4 × 4 (Rover 9),** 1962, U.K.

155 **Truck, Fire Fighting, $\frac{3}{4}$ ton, 4 × 4, Land Rover,** 1960, U.K.

156 **Truck, Cab Forward, Fire Fighting, 1 ton, 4 × 4, Land Rover,** 1965, U.K.

157 **Truck, GS, $\frac{3}{4}$ ton, with Rapier Ground-to-air Missile Launching Fire and Power Unit,** 1969, U.K.

158 **Rapier Missile, Fire, Power and Tracking Units,** 1969, U.K.

159 **Truck, 4 × 4, $\frac{1}{2}$ ton, GS, Lightweight Air Portable, Land Rover,** 1969, U.K.

160 **Truck, Cargo, 1 ton, 4 × 4, Land Rover, Forward Control,** 1966, U.K.

The famous Land Rover was introduced in 1949 as a four-wheel-drive field car

for the sort of duties that the Jeep had performed in World War II. Built with both commercial and military markets in mind it was soon adopted for service with the British Army, Navy and Air Force, and for literally dozens of other fighting services the world over. With the demise of the Austin Champ which had originally been planned as a Jeep replacement by the British Army, the Land Rover became even more widely used and numerous special purpose variants appeared in the late 1950s and the 1960s. In 1960 a series 2 model was introduced with slightly revised bodywork.

The standard $\frac{1}{4}$-ton (later $\frac{1}{2}$-ton) model had an 88 in. wheelbase while the $\frac{3}{4}$-ton model has a 109 in. wheelbase. The basic Rover 8 has the 88 in. wheelbase and a Rover four-cylinder engine. It differs from commercial models in having twin fuel tanks, lashing eyes and cleats, modified bumpers, military pattern tow hook and tyres, military type headlamps and reinforced rear chassis. It also has mounting points for a radio in the back. Plate 151 shows a Rover 8 used by the Australian Army, fitted with a U.S.-built M40A1 recoilless rifle (demountable) and with locally modified mudguards that have their length reduced in front. The drawing shows the side doors and windscreen removed, a design feature of the vehicle which can be so modified as desired to suit active service conditions.

The $\frac{3}{4}$-ton model (Rover 9) has the 109-in. wheelbase, and is modified from its commercial equivalent as for the Rover 8. This vehicle is used as a gun tractor for the 105-mm pack howitzer in Parachute Field Regiments of the Royal Artillery, both the vehicle and the gun being air-portable. In infantry battalions it acts as carrier for the Wombat recoilless anti-tank gun (Plate 152) with a sliding ramp for use in loading or off-loading the weapon. The Wombat can also be fired from the vehicle.

Both the short and long wheelbase Land Rovers are also used in FFR (fitted for radio) form in which guise it has a rectified 24-volt instead of 12-volt electrical system, full suppression, a wireless table, aerial brackets, two extra batteries and provision for battery charging.

Certain arms, including Bomb Disposal and other technical branches, use the 'Utility' version of the Land Rover (Plate 153) which is basically a commercial long wheelbase model with fibreglass hardtop and extra side doors. This model is also used by the RN and RAF and for miscellaneous non-combatant roles by many other armed forces.

On the Rover 9 chassis a well-known special type is the ambulance (Plate 154) which is intended specifically for front line work. Bodywork on this vehicle is entirely of aluminium with thermal insulation and offers accommodation for two stretchers or one stretcher and three seated wounded, or six seated wounded.

For the RAF there is a special version of the long wheelbase Land Rover (Plate 155) as a fire fighting and rescue vehicle for airfields. The conversion is by the well-known fire engine makers, Merryweather, and the equipment added includes dry chemical powder to combat aircraft fire. Nitrogen is used to discharge the powder, and this is carried in cylinders. The powder itself is in two 200-lb containers. Floodlamps, a light ladder, tools and cutting equipment and two 75 ft hand hoses attached to the powder containers complete the fittings.

The Army Fire Service uses a special version of the Forward Control Land Rover (Plate 156) which carries conventional fire fighting equipment including hoses, water and foam extinguishers, and rescue tools for use in base installations. This vehicle is designated officially as 'Truck, Cab Forward, Fire Fighting'.

The Forward Control Land Rover itself (Plate 160) is used only in small numbers for miscellaneous duties by the British Army, but in 1970 a special militarised version of this 1-tonner was under development, differing slightly from the original commercial design. However, the basic design was also available for export sales to other military forces.

The most recent new role for the Land Rover emphasising its importance as a lightweight air-portable type, is as a tractor unit for the new Rapier missile system. The Rapier is a tactical guided weapon designed to be both inexpensive, simple to operate, and flexible in operational use. It is intended for combatting low flying supersonic and ground attack aircraft and is broken down into three parts—the Fire Unit, Power Unit, and Tracker Unit for deployment (Plate 158). The tracker and power units link up to form a single trailer for towing, and tracker unit is carried in the Land Rover together with missile 're-loads' (Plate 157). The compactness of the system is apparent from the drawings.

The relatively small size of the Land Rover and the Rapier system makes handling and concealment easy, while the entire system is air-portable, thus conforming to the most important of modern military requirements. Only one man is needed to operate the system and a full detachment consists of three men, a major saving in manpower compared with, say, the Bofors gun used in an air defence role. The Rapier system employs a radar to scan the horizon and an optical tracking system to sight and control the missile after the target is acquired.

The most recent development of the Land Rover carries the air-portability qualities of the vehicle to their logical conclusion. This is a special lightweight model developed specially for military use. Essentially it is a stripped down version of the short wheelbase Land Rover with all non-essentials omitted, and all fittings (e.g. hood, body sides, doors, windscreen, bumpers, and spare wheel) easily detachable for loading in aircraft or helicopters. Plate 159 shows it both fully equipped and stripped for a helicopter lift by an RAF Wessex helicopter. Rated at $\frac{1}{2}$ ton, the design is rather more rugged and serviceable than earlier models and it will eventually replace the older Rovers in service use. It is being produced in both cargo and FFR versions like earlier models. A 2·25-litre four-cylinder engine is standard and when stripped down the vehicle weighs little more than a ton. Overall length is 12 ft, overall width is 5 ft, and overall height (with canvas tilt) is 6 ft 5 in.

161 **Car, Light, 4 × 2, Morris 1000 Traveller**
162 **Car, Medium, 4 × 2, Austin 1800**
163 **Car, Medium, 4 × 2, Ford Zephyr,** 1960–70, U.K.

These three cars are typical of standard commercial products purchased for military use. Apart from their military colour schemes they are identical to stock vehicles. Cars are used for a number of routine military duties such as staff transport, senior officers' transport, courier, and police or traffic control work. The first two vehicles here (Plates 161 and 162) are in the markings of a bomb disposal squad based in Britain where most of the movement takes place over public roads and thus cars make a perfectly convenient mode of transport. They have orange warning beacons like public service vehicles for use in emergencies. The Ford Zephyr is typical of the transport used by staff and senior officers, and is representative of equivalent types of car used by all armed forces for this task.

164 **Tractor, Wheeled, 6 × 6, 20 ton, Scammell Super Constructor, with 50–60 ton Semi-trailer Tank Transporter, Crane-Fruehauf**
166 **Tractor, Wheeled, 6 × 6, Scammell Super Constructor with Ballast Body,** 1968, U.K.

This is an example of a standard commercial vehicle and trailer built in Britain and sold abroad to several military authorities. This particular equipment was not supplied to the British Army. The prime mover has a pedigree going right back to the Scammell Pioneer of pre-war days. A Rolls-Royce C6 12-litre 275 b.h.p. oil engine provides the power for this vehicle and a power take-off also drives a 15-ton capacity winch mounted behind the cab to assist in loading the trailer or for recovery purposes. The tractor unit has six wheel drive with an articulated balance beam rear bogie, as used in earlier Scammell models, and there is a pre-selector automatic gearbox. Power-assisted steering is another feature. The tractor is 10 ft high and 10 ft 10 in. wide, with a wheelbase of 17 ft 2½ in. The empty weight of the unit is 32,480 lbs.

The Crane Fruehauf 50–60 tank transporter semi-trailer used with this outfit is 38 ft 7½ in. long and is of the girder frame type—cranked to fit the prime mover coupling unit. The decking is of mild steel welded to the frame members. The rear suspension is of the unsprung rocker beam type with eight twin-wheel bogies (16 wheels in all) mounted in four rows on four axles. The steel axles have roller bearing hubs. This semi-trailer is 11 ft wide and 8 ft 7 in. high. It is designed specifically for carrying tanks of up to 50 tons, in particular the Centurion (shown) or the M47/M48 Patton series. Stores and small vehicles of up to this equivalent weight can also be carried. Major customers for this vehicle and transporter unit include South Africa, Israel, Jordan and other Middle East states. Laden weight of the semi-trailer with Centurion tank is about 170,000 lbs. Empty weight of the semi-trailer is 35,728 lbs.

165 **Tractor, Wheeled, 6 × 6, 20 ton, Scammell Contractor, with 50–60-ton Semi-trailer Tank Transporter, Crane-Fruehauf,** 1968, U.K.

The Contractor is virtually a refined version of the Constructor designed to offer a wide range of alternative engines, gearboxes, and even suspension units to suit the requirements of individual customers. Though built in Britain by Scammell Lorries Ltd. this vehicle is not

166

used by the British Army but is offered for sale to overseas nations.

In addition the Contractor is also sold in various commercial forms for long range road haulage. In military configuration the Contractor is sold as a prime mover for the Crane Fruehauf 50–60-ton semi-trailer tank transporter (see previous entry) in which form it is illustrated, carrying a Centurion tank. Alternatives include a tractor with ballast body for towing full trailers, a recovery and breakdown tractor, or a long wheelbase rigid chassis high capacity cargo truck. The number of options offered means that in most cases the purchaser can specify engines and mechanical parts to match those which may already be standardised within the rest of his transport fleet.

A typical power unit would be a Cummins six-cylinder diesel unit of 335 b.h.p. air brakes, a hydraulic clutch and a Fuller gearbox with 12 forward and two reverse ratios would be provided. The Contractor has a wide bonnet allowing most available power units of suitable type to be accommodated.

167 **Tractor, Heavy Recovery, 6 × 6, Scammell Super 90 Constructor,** 1966, U.K.

This vehicle was a modernised version of the Scammell 6 × 6 recovery vehicle shown in Plate 137. It was similar in all respects except that it incorporated the cab and some mechanical parts of the Super Constructor series. This model did not go into service with the British Army but was supplied for export with a range of power units to suit the needs of individual customers. The drawing illustrates very well the flexibility of the famous Scammell suspension system which gives these vehicles the excellent cross-country performance. The chain and rubber tracks, similar to the old WD pattern, give added traction in muddy conditions. The roof 'convoy' hatch and insulating canopy are fittings for overseas military service.

168 Tractor, Wheeled, 6 × 6, 20 ton, Scammell Contractor with Ballast Body, 1968, U.K.

Another type supplied for export, and not actually used by the British Army, is a ballast body version of the vehicle shown in Plate 165. This is used primarily for towing a 50-ton full trailer tank transporter or a machinery carrier. This vehicle is also sold commercially. There is a range of engine options to suit individual customer requirements. Vehicles in the Contractor and Super Constructor range have been supplied to several countries who traditionally have bought military vehicles from Britain, including South Africa and Jordan.

169 Airfield Fire Tender, 6 × 6, Thornycroft Nubian, Mk VII, 1966, U.K.

This distinctive vehicle is widely used by the British Royal Air Force as a standard airfield fire tender and crash truck, and came into service in the early 1960s. It is also used by the British Army Fire Service and has been sold all over the world to other armies and air forces. Sold also commercially, it is used by many civil airport authorities. The vehicle is built on the Thornycroft TFA B81 6 × 6 chassis which has a Rolls-Royce B81 engine of 235 b.h.p. Actual design of the body work and fittings was undertaken by the Pyrene Co., the major firefighting appliance manufacturers. The principal feature is the roof-mounted dual output foam monitor which is supplied from a 110 gallon foam compound tank and a 700 gallon water tank carried within the vehicle. There is a 'blower unit' to mix the constituents and generate the foam. In addition to the monitor there are four hand hoses connected to the foam unit. The unit is so arranged that for lengthy operations extra water and foam compound can be pumped in from an adjacent vehicle without disturbing output. Crew of the vehicle is four.

170 Truck, Cargo, 4 × 4, 3 ton, Bedford RL
171 Thunderbird, High-level Air Defence Missile
172 Truck, Cargo, 4 × 4, Air portable, Dropside Bedford RL, with 3-ton Transportable Container
173 Truck-mounted Repair Shop, 4 × 4, 3 ton Bedford RL, 1955–70, U.K.

In the early 1950s new 3-ton vehicles started to enter service as replacements for the wartime 3-tonners which soldiered on, in some cases until 1960 or beyond. Ford, Commer and Bedford all received contracts. All designs incorporated as many commercial parts as possible. Ultimately Vauxhall (Bedford) became the major producers and the Bedford RL 3-tonner became almost as familiar as the wartime Bedfords. It remained in production until at least

1969, being replaced by yet another Bedford model. The Bedford RL is a perfectly straightforward adaptation of the basic Bedford 7-ton commercial chassis. The additions include a rear winch mounted in the chassis and giving a 2½-ton pull. The steel cab is a slightly modified version of the ordinary commercial cab.

In its basic cargo form (Plate 170) with steel general service body, the Bedford is 20 ft 10 in. long, 10 ft high, and 7 ft 9 in. wide. It has dropsides, and folding bench seats for personnel. Permitted top speed is 35 m.p.h. Very many variants exist on this chassis, including a cargo truck with Atlas hydraulic crane for handling palletted stores and ammunition. There is also an airportable version (Plate 172) with removable cab roof to permit close stowage with other equipment in the confines of an aircraft hold. A bulk fuel tanker, mobile repair shop (Plate 173), mobile dental clinic, end tipper, light breakdown truck, and a wireless truck are all also produced on the same chassis.

The most recent development with this vehicle is the use of truck transportable containers which are made in standard panels so that a layout of doors and windows can be selected for a given role. The panels are made of aluminium to keep weight to the minimum. A typical arrangement is shown in the drawing. Canvas side screens are fitted as necessary to form penthouse extensions. Jacks below the container support it when it is being changed—the vehicle simply drives out and leaves the container standing on its legs.

One task of the Bedford 4 × 4 is as a towing behicle for the Thunderbird guided missile, shown on its transport

trailer (Plate 171). This very flexible weapons system was designed from the start with a high degree of portability so that launching sites can be rapidly changed in a fast-moving tactical situation. All parts of the missile and its equipment break down into conveniently sized loads.

In 1969 the existing 3-ton truck range was re-rated to 4 tons and re-designated accordingly.

174 **Class 30 Trackway (portable roadway) mounted on Truck, Cargo, Dropside, 4 × 4, 3 ton, Bedford RL,** 1966, U.K.

The Class 30 Trackway (popularly called the Saro Trackway) and its larger derivative, the Class 60 Trackway, are widely used, particularly in amphibious work. The Class 30 portable roadway system consist of flexibly joined aluminium alloy 'planks' 11 ft wide and 150 ft 9 in. long. The Class 60 roadway comes in two sizes, 15 ft and 7½ ft wide and is usually pre-assembled in 25 ft lengths for joining to other lengths on site. The Class 30 Trackway is used for wheeled and light tracked vehicles and can be launched off its spool and recovered later by the carrier vehicle. It is normally carried on its spool all mounted on a turntable so that it is simply swung across the axis of the carrier vehicle for launching. A roller frame assembly is erected to form a launching guide. The most usual carrier vehicle is the Bedford 3–4-tonner shown, but the same equipment can be carried and launched from other vehicles, notably the Michigan DS75 Tractor. The total weight of a 150 ft trackway length (Class 30) is 9,298 lbs. The Class 60 track weighs 105 lb per foot used. This latter is, of course, intended to make a roadway over the beach for tanks and other very heavy vehicles.

175 Rough Terrain Fork Lift Tractor, Eager Beaver, 1967, U.K.

This little vehicle is typical of the types which meet the latest requirements in military transport demanding versatility as well as portability by air. The Eager Beaver was designed from the start to fit comfortably inside existing military transport aircraft even the Hawker Siddeley Andover, the smallest conventional load carrier in RAF service. The vehicle combines the two functions of fork lift truck and tractor for work either on advanced airstrips, parachute dropping zones, or in engineers' field squadrons. For its relatively low weight of 6,100 lbs it has a very high load capacity (4,000 lbs) and a powerful engine giving a maximum speed of 40 m.p.h. Its four-cylinder Perkins diesel engine gives 78 b.h.p. at 2,500 r.p.m. The vehicle has four-wheel drive and four-wheel steering giving a 30 ft turning circle.

A single beam mast with hydraulic lift fitted at the front can carry either forks (for handling palletted loads) or a gantry. For storage in an aircraft, the mast tilts back 20° to reduce overall height.

To go with the Eager Beaver in its tractor role is a 5 ton air-portable trailer, of which two can be hauled when fully loaded. The trailer is designed to be taken apart for easy stowage in an aircraft. For a rapid turn round of a transport aircraft on a forward strip several Eager Beavers would operate with 'trains' of trailers, some vehicles loading the trailers and others towing the loaded trailers to the stores area.

The Eager Beaver could operate unprepared in water up to 30 in. deep. It is 17 ft 9 in. long and 6 ft wide. The chassis is of space frame tubular construction and bodywork is largely omitted to save weight.

176 Tracked Carrier, Volvo BV 200, 1968, Sweden/U.K.

This novel light weight Swedish articulated tracked vehicle has been widely adopted, and the British Army uses it as a snow vehicle instead of the old Weasel (Plate 123). The very wide rubber tracks and light weight give a very low ground pressure making it specially suitable for operating on snow, ice, mud or swampland. The permanently coupled trailer is driven via a flexible shaft from the engine in the tractor unit. The Volvo can carry 10–12 men or stores in the trailer unit.

177 Tractor, Wheeled, GS, 20 ton, 6 × 6, Scammell, 1962, U.K.

A modified version of the tractor shown in Plate 134, this vehicle differs mainly in having a more powerful Rolls Royce C6 engine of 184 b.h.p. and a re-designed cab. It can tow a 30-ton low loading trailer for engineering plant or a normal cargo trailer. Apart from being used by the British Army it is also used by the RAF and is shown here as a stores support vehicle for the Harrier VTOL aircraft at a forward landing ground.

178 **Truck, 5 ton, Cargo, High Mobility Load Carrier, 6 × 6, Alvis Stalwart Mk 2,** 1966, U.K.

The Stalwart started as a 'private venture' by Alvis in 1960 and was envisaged for both military and commercial use, in the latter case as an exploration vehicle for oil companies and the like. The military value of the Stalwart was obvious and after military trials, which led to a few minor production changes, the vehicle went into production for the British Army. The first vehicles in service were designated Mk 1 and had small cab windows and was less powerful in the water. The definitive production version is the Mk 2, with enlarged windows to give better vision. The Stalwart is used exclusively as a stores and supply carrier for armoured divisions, used mainly to follow up the tanks with more fuel and ammunition. The Stalwart can go virtually anywhere that the tanks go. A further variant has an Atlas hydraulic crane for handling ammunition and is used as a limber vehicle for the Abbot SP gun.

The unique feature of the Stalwart is its ability to cross rough country using its six-wheel chassis layout, and also its amphibious qualities. Propulsion in the water is effected by 2 Dowty marine jet units which take in and eject water at pressure to give forward movement. Vanes are fitted in the propulsion units for steering. If the propulsion system fails the road wheels can be used for both crude steering and water propulsion. All wheels are independently sprung and the vehicle can cross 5 ft trenches and climb 1 in 3 slopes. The vehicle is 20 ft 10¼ in. long, 8 ft 7 in. wide, and 8 ft 10 in. high.

INDEX

This index is arranged broadly by type or function under 13 headings so that all vehicles illustrated in a particular category (e.g. Transport Vehicles) can be turned up quickly by reference to the relevant list. Multi-role vehicles appear here more than once, under every appropriate heading. Details of dates of service are given in the text and are not listed here. When dates are given in text headings for a group of vehicles they refer to the general period of service and not necessarily to every vehicle shown in the group. Country of origin, and any major secondary user or users are also indicated in the text headings (e.g. Sweden/U.K.). In many cases, however, vehicles were used by dozens of countries (e.g. the Jeep) and the countries indicated generally refer to the actual example drawn.

For simplicity, cross-references in the text are made to plate numbers only, though reference should also be made to the corresponding descriptive text where relevant.

7 SPECIAL BODIED TYPES (Vans, Offices, Cranes, Tankers, etc.)

8 RECOVERY, BREAKDOWN, PRIME MOVER and TANK TRANSPORTER VEHICLES, and TRAILERS